PRINCIPLES
of
POLICE INTERROGATION

PRINCIPLES
of
POLICE INTERROGATION

By

C. H. VAN METER
Lieutenant
Orlando Police Department
Orlando, Florida

With a Foreword by

William J. Bopp

CHARLES C THOMAS · PUBLISHER
Springfield · Illinois · U.S.A.

Published and Distributed Throughout the World by
CHARLES C THOMAS · PUBLISHER
BANNERSTONE HOUSE
301-327 East Lawrence Avenue, Springfield, Illinois, U.S.A.

© *1973, by* CHARLES C THOMAS · PUBLISHER
ISBN 0-398-02634-3
Library of Congress Catalog Card Number: 72-84150

With THOMAS BOOKS *careful attention is given to all details of
manufacturing and design. It is the Publisher's desire to present books
that are satisfactory as to their physical qualities and artistic possibilities
and appropriate for their particular use.* THOMAS BOOKS *will be true
to those laws of quality that assure a good name and good will.*

Printed in the United States of America
H-2

FOREWORD

U<small>NITED</small> S<small>TATES</small> Supreme Court decisions of the last two decades, coupled with a rapidly changing social environment, have contributed to a lessening of public confidence in certain police practices. One such practice is the *police interrogation*. Several landmark court decisions have been aimed at strengthening individual liberties by weakening the right of law enforcement officers to detain, question, and elicit confessions from criminal suspects. With all the legal restrictions now imposed on the police, and with a steadily rising rate of serious crimes, it is essential that the police effectively utilize those crime-fighting tools at their disposal, while remaining cautious that they do not misuse them, thus inviting restrictive court action.

To those civil libertarians who would view police questioning of criminal suspects as an evil in itself, one can but hope that it is not their daughter who is raped or their wife who is assaulted. The police have a right to interrogate suspects and it will be a sad day for the country if that right were taken away or limited beyond its present state. Interrogation is an art, a device designed as much for releasing the innocent as convicting the guilty, and a method by which the public can be safeguarded against crime.

It is always pleasing when a professional practitioner with the knowledge and experience of Lieutenant C. H. Van Meter decides to synthesize his experiences into a published work, especially when the area about which he writes is a police subject that frightens some people and is frequently misunderstood—often purposely—by others. In this work, Lieutenant Van Meter presents material that is candid, honest, and completely consistent with constitutional and ethical considerations. It should be of value to working police officers, regardless of rank or assignment, and to criminal justice students whose career pursuits are either in the area of law enforcement or in closely related fields such as parole, probation, and corrections.

W<small>ILLIAM</small> J. B<small>OPP</small>

PREFACE

THE history of interrogation probably dates back to the time when Adam asked, "Are you sure it's all right to pick the apple?" With that long a history, there should be no mystery left about interrogation. However, I believe there is at least as much misunderstanding in the field of interrogation as there is in any other area of police work. To someone who through the school of hard knocks has learned the basic "how-to's," interrogation is only a process of learning new techniques; but to someone new to the craft, interrogation appears to be something of a formidable barrier. My effort herein, therefore, will not be to present techniques, but to acquaint the newcomer with a few suggestions and ideas of how to approach the field of interrogation with a certain amount of confidence.

Interrogation is basically a contact between someone who possibly possesses some undisclosed information and someone else who wants to know this undisclosed information. In police work, a great many cases are resolved by an interrogator who utilizes the case history and evidence, and uses proper interrogative technique, thus causing the suspect to confess to his part in the affair or to his knowledge of the incident.

Most contacts in police work involve interviews, not interrogations. Probably the best definition of interview is "A conversation with a purpose." When you interview someone, you direct the conversation and gather the facts as spoken by the person, without objecting or causing the person to think that you do not believe him. Interviews are generally cordial and rather informally structured, there being no adverse relationship between the principals. In the interrogation field, the primary purpose is to elicit an admission or at least the truth; occasionally, this necessitates causing the suspect to believe that you don't think he's telling the truth. Certainly, if someone up and told you, "You're lying," you probably wouldn't tell him the time of day from that time on. However, by using basic interrogation techniques, approaches, and ideas it is possible to tell the suspect he's lying in such a manner as to make him think you're doing him a favor. It's not as difficult as it sounds, either. If the interrogator is equipped with a basic understanding of human nature and applies this to some sound fundamental interrogation principles, he can successfully conclude many cases that would otherwise have gone unresolved.

This volume is designed to present to the beginning interrogator or the law enforcement student, a perspective on how to prepare for the interrogation, how to start the conversation, how to keep it going, what to do when you come to the end, and some basic ideas to be mindful of when coming into contact with the person to be interrogated. A suspect usually has no reason to come right out and tell you anything. The task of the interrogator is to cause the suspect to think that he should tell you, the interrogator, whatever information you might be seeking. It's not that difficult! The very first thing you have going for you is that man is a social animal; he does not want to live alone. He must be part of life and wants to be with other people. This basic urge to be part of the human race is the basic advantage that the interrogator has over the suspect. Through the application of the proper psychological pressures (consistent with constitutional and ethical limitations) on this suspect, he will confess, provided that you, the interrogator, do the right thing at the right time, and provided, of course, that he is guilty. No less important to the ethical interrogator is the release of an innocent man from custody.

Interrogation is described in the following ways:

To examine by asking questions.

Synonyms: ask, inquire, search, examine.

To learn facts and to obtain admissions or confessions of wrongful acts.

To question topically with formality, command, and thoroughness for full information and circumstantial detail.

It all adds up to the fact that you want the guilty party to confess his crime to you. This interpersonal contact can be, and oftentimes is, the most crucial part of a criminal investigation. Many cases would have remained unsolved if it were not for some interrogator eliciting a confession, thereby closing the case. Can you, the beginner, teach yourself how to be this kind of interrogator? Certainly! Not without work and practice, however. This book will attempt to explain how to get started, how to open the door to interrogation. Practice and reading more advanced books on this subject will teach you how to become more proficient in the art. But you have to make a start. This book is designed to get you off the blocks and started down the track. The ideas are not exclusively my inventions. The suggestions are not necessarily of my own imagination. This business of interrogation is an old one. This book has tried to bring enough basic facts together to give the beginner a basic introduction to the mysteries of interrogation.

The police field cannot have too many good interrogators. The sad fact now is that there are too few really good, imaginative interrogators. You can associate yourself, by your own efforts and thoughts, with the very best professionals in the business if you just make the start.

I have often heard that General Custer told his men, "Don't take any prisoners." However, police departments do take prisoners and it is up to you and me, the interrogators, to determine if the suspect has some undisclosed knowledge. If he does, we want him to confess. How do we get him to do this? I hope this book will be of some help along these lines.

C. H. VAN METER

ACKNOWLEDGMENTS

Honorable Warren H. Edwards, Senior Judge, Criminal Court of Record for Orange County, Florida. His help, advice, and experience were extremely valuable in establishing form and layout for statements, plus he gave support and encouragement over the years.

Meredith J. Cohen, Attorney at Law, Orlando, Florida. His view from both sides, the prosecution and the defense, plus his review and suggestions in this book, were invaluable in its preparation.

William J. Bopp, Assistant Professor and Coordinator, Law Enforcement Program, Florida Technological University, Orlando, Florida. The business of finishing this book would have proven overwhelming without the advice and help and support so freely given.

My wife, for her long hours of typing, proofreading, and encouragement during the entire preparation.

Mr. Leonard Harrelson, Director, Keeler Polygraph Institute, Chicago, Illinois, and Dr. Richard C. Steinmetz, Instructor at Keeler, for my first real look at interrogation as an art.

C. H. V. M.

CONTENTS

PRINCIPLES
of
POLICE INTERROGATION

Chapter 1

HISTORY OF INTERROGATION PREPAREDNESS

One man's word is no man's word; we should
quietly hear both sides.

—GOETHE

THE history of interrogation dates to the dawn of history. Any act
of questioning another can be considered interrogation. However,
since the formation of laws to regulate man, and since the formation
of a group to enforce these laws, the term interrogation has been
principally associated with the enforcer of the law questioning the
violator of the law. Not much is written on the history of interrogation, when it started, or who first began to give the interrogation
techniques the dignity of preplanning. Yet, it is not inconceivable
that the act of interrogation has played an important part in the
solution of most every major case in the history of man. Metternich
states that "The men who make history have not time to write it."
It is unfortunate that some of the better interrogators in the past have
not written down their theories and practices for the benefit of those
who have followed.

I have read that in ancient Arabia, one form of interrogation was
to inform each suspect that he would be sent into a tent where he
would find a sacred donkey. Once inside, he was to pull the donkey's
tail and the sacred donkey would bray only when the guilty party
pulled the tail. The trick, however, was that lampblack was placed
on the donkey's tail. The innocent parties, believing the story of the
donkey, would enter, pull the tail, and as a result get lampblack on
their hands. The hope was that the innocent would pull the tail and
the guilty party would not. I can see as many holes in this theory
as you can, but I suppose that without better education on the subject, it was their best effort to bring about a solution to some un-

[3]

resolved crime. Another method, one used by the Chinese, was to place dried rice in the mouths of the suspects. If the rice became moist, it was assumed that the suspect was innocent, for a guilty party's mouth is usually dry. Again, the margin for error is tremendous, and there is no protection at all for the suspects being so tried.

It is quite apparent that appreciations of human behavior are present in both of these methods of seeking the guilty party. In the Arabian method, they knew human nature well enough to know that the guilty party would not touch the tail of the donkey, thereby avoiding detection. Since the person was in the tent alone, the Arabs probably occasionally got their guilty man. In the Chinese method, it is a known physiological fact that a person under extreme tension ordinarily will have a dry mouth. There are physiological and psychological explanations for this fact, and thus the Chinese too occasionally got the right man.

Both of the old methods indicate that a great deal of observation went into devising them. It is not my purpose to criticize these devices, but only to recognize the fact that for many hundreds of years, man has been attempting to discover some method of determining the truth. By reading and learning from the old methods and theories, and by applying their basic ideas to our situation and incorporating the new advances in psychology and physiology to our present-day situations, we can advance this art of interrogation. One cannot interrogate or advance interrogation if he just sits on his hands. He must work and learn and put the information into action. Don't be like the story of Pat and Mary who took their difficulties to court. They had been fighting and the judge asked, "Pat, I understand you and Mary had some words." "Yes, I had some," said Pat, "but I didn't get to use mine."

If you intend to be an interrogator, you can't let it be said that you didn't get to use your words. You have to learn from the past, learn what others have written on the subject, and put them to use. There is no such thing as a born interrogator. Every man who has been successful in this field has had to learn the basic concepts of the art and then test them. Practice may not make you the perfect interrogator, but practice will make you a confident, efficient interrogator.

I have heard it said that we often wonder why men lie about each other when the plain truth would be bad enough. So you are going to try to put yourself in the position of being able to get other men to tell the truth. It is a big undertaking and one not to be lightly considered. It can be done, and will be done, if you apply the proper foundation to your learning and technique, and learn from others how to get started. By learning the basic fundamentals of how to get started, you cannot fail to build and develop your ability to become a really good interrogator.

And so into the book. I have tried to break it up into usable parts and steps so that you can get the entire picture of the idea as it unfolds.

Chapter 2

CASE PREPAREDNESS

THE BEST way to begin any interrogation is to prepare yourself before you ever meet the subject with whom you plan to talk. One big mistake made by some interrogators is to stride into an interrogation unprepared. If you go in unprepared, you can only bluff. If you don't know all the facts of the case, you can't intelligently pursue any reasonable line of questioning, coupled with the fact that you really don't know if the subject is lying or not as he responds to your conversation. Never walk in cold if you can help it.

To be properly prepared to interrogate requires effort on your part. You never will learn about any case by just standing by and listening to the investigating officers talk about the case at random. A good interrogator is also a good investigator in his fact gathering. A good interrogator must work at preparing himself with the proper background of the case: the facts, times, places, who, what, why, when, and so forth. Never take anything for granted. Check for yourself if possible. Good interrogators are doers; they are not like the fellow who was asked by another, "Why did the Chief fire you?" Said he, "Well, the Chief is the man who stands around and watches others work." "Yes, but why did the Chief fire *you?*" He replied, "He got jealous of me. A lot of the fellows thought I was the Chief."

I feel that it is best to have some method for this fact gathering; some idea or checklist to follow when you begin to analyze the information that you need to know to intelligently interrogate a suspect. I have found that a very useful first contact with the case is a short "interrogation request" report. If you are not in a position to ask for this report, it is still a good idea to keep this form in mind, and mentally fill it out as you talk to the investigators. This short synopsis of the crime will often condense the information into a few short sentences so that you can grasp the case in total. You can get a picture of the whole case and can then direct your search for information along the lines that will be most productive and useful to you in the interrogation room.

Figure 1 represents a blank request form that I have found to be most successful for my purpose. Most of the spaces on the form can be completed without explanation. There are a few, however, that require some explanation as to what I expect to be filled in. Follow the form and I will explain them briefly.

Name of person and office making request. Often, the person requesting the interrogation and the investigating officers are different people. It is important to know all the people involved in the case so that if you need more information or facts you can contact all the people having some knowledge of the case.

FIGURE 1

REQUEST FOR INTERROGATION

TO:_____Police Dept.   Date_____

Name of Person and Office making request:_____

Subject's Name_____

Race_____Sex_____DOB_____FBI RECORD: Yes____No_____

Has subject been previously interrogated? If so, explain:_____

_____

Nature of Investigation:_____

Felony_____Misdemeanor_____Defendant or Witness_____

Name of officer in charge of case:_____

Brief statement of facts regarding case:_____

_____

_____

_____

_____

Requested By
_____

Title & Dept.

Subject's name. Self-explanatory.

Race. Self-explanatory. Often, depending on a person's race and/or education, an interrogator will have to suit his conversation and word usage to the subject's, so that some understanding is achieved.

Sex. Self-explanatory.

DOB. Date of birth. Again, the conversation and word usage will have to suit the age of the subject.

FBI record. This you should check yourself.

Has subject been previously interrogated? If he has, be careful. You will have to check when, by whom, how long, and so on. If someone has just walked out of the interrogation room after a four- or five-hour session, you don't stand much of a chance if you go right in. Not only that, but marathon interrogations are not favorably accepted by the courts, and so, even if you got the confession, you would have a difficult time using the information. Remember, if a person tells a lie and then successfully repeats and repeats it, each retelling reinforces his ability to lie. If a suspect sees that he has beaten one interrogator by lying, he will find it much easier to lie to each succeeding interrogator. Give yourself and the suspect a break and allow him to rest and eat and even sleep, if that is in order. To allow the subject the human rights of rest and proper comforts is not only humanitarian, but will show him that you have his welfare at heart. It also allows him time to dwell on the facts of the crime, and quite often makes your job as interrogator easier if his conscience has been active. All-day grilling sessions are archaic and absolutely unnecessary. Anyone who resorts to these tactics is a detriment to the law enforcement profession. He is exhibiting his own inadequacies and does nothing to promote the profession of law enforcement and the art of interrogation. Discover who has talked to this subject and what, if anything, he has found out. It might be helpful to you. Determine from any previous interrogators just how much the suspect knows about the crime and how much they told him.

Nature of investigation. Listed here are possible charges that will be made if, in fact, the subject is responsible.

Felony/misdemeanor. Self-explanatory.

Defendant or witness. By knowing in what category this suspect falls, you can best direct your conversation.

Name of officer in charge of case. As in the case of the requester, you might need to refer to the knowledgeable people in the case, and therefore, need to know who to contact.

Brief statement of facts regarding case. A short, concise, synopsis of the case.

All of the foregoing information is important for the interrogator to know during his preliminary preparation for the case. The form itself need not be used, but obtain the information for your own benefit. By being armed with this short history, you will be better able to know what information will be valuable to you as you study other reports on the case and you search for evidence and other items of importance that will be listed. You cannot know too much about the case before you walk into the interrogation room. You *can* know too little, and when you fall short, the subject knows it and you cannot do your job thoroughly.

Now that we have a general understanding of the case and have in mind exactly what we are looking for and what we expect to get from the subject, the next logical step is to determine as much information about the subject as we have available to us. Certainly, the more we know about the subject, the better prepared we will be to start the conversation, and then to pursue this subject's thoughts, motivations, ideas, and so forth. Also, if we can determine this subject's background and education prior to talking to him, we can key our words and conversation to his level of understanding.

Figure 2 is the form utilized by the Orlando Police Department to gather background information from the subject during the mugging and printing period. As you know, most departments take photographs and fingerprints when a person is first arrested as a suspect for some offense. During the photographing and fingerprinting (mugging and printing) session, it is very easy to include the form and have the identification officer fill it out and maintain it as part of this suspect's permanent record. In this department, the form is affectionately called the "pedigree" sheet to keep it separated from the "rap" sheet, the Federal Bureau of Investigation's information form.

FIGURE 2
PRISONER DESCRIPTION FORM

Record No._____   **POLICE DEPARTMENT**   FPC_____

Date of Record_____

IDENTIFICATION BUREAU
Prisoner's Description
New ☐   Repeater ☐

Name	First	Middle	Last					Address

Alias _____

COLOR	SEX	AGE	HEIGHT	WEIGHT	HAIR	EYES	COMPLEXION
BUILD	FORMER ADDRESS			BIRTH DATE	BIRTHPLACE		
OCCUPATION				EMPLOYED BY			
MARITAL STATUS			DESCENT				

Name	Address	City	State
HUSBAND OR WIFE			
FATHER OR INLAWS			
MOTHER			
BROTHER			
BROTHER			
SISTER			
SISTER			
FRIEND			
FRIEND			

Scars, Marks, Deformities	Tattoos
Education GS ☐ HS ☐ Coll. ☐	Speech
Religion Prot. ☐ Cath. ☐ Others ☐	Remarks
Prev. Arrests Yes ☐ No ☐	
U. S. Serv.	
U. S. Serv. No.	IN	OUT	
Type of Discharge	
Smokes	
Drinks	RECORD TAKEN BY

Review this sheet now as we go over some of the high points, and you will soon see that this is a veritable storehouse of information about the subject to be interrogated. By learning the facts listed on this sheet prior to talking to the suspect, some of the newness or strangeness of the subject disappears, and he becomes more of an acquaintance rather than a total stranger. By knowing some of his background, it is more like talking to a friend than to someone whom you have never met. Each of us is a little shy with new acquaintances, but as we come to know the person the conversation is easier and the feelings on both sides are not as awkward as time passes. It is human nature to be a little bashful, and therefore, if we arm ourselves with as much background on the subject as is available, we overcome this feeling, even before we meet the subject.

Some of the information will be repetitious, but still important to note in determining if the subject is relating a consistent story to all people that he comes into contact with. As we look down this sheet, we notice that his age, height, weight, and phsyical description is included. All of us know that there are some personality character- istics usually attributed to physical attributes. Fat men are not always jolly but they are always fat, and usually very conscious of the fact. The interrogator, therefore, trys to avoid any conversation that would suggest this problem to the suspect, avoids discussion of physical prowess that the suspect could not possibly possess, and avoids dis- cussion of his being attractive physically. One of the best ways to lose an interrogation is to alienate the suspect by some indiscreet remark that will offend him. You can discuss a fat man's intel- ligence, disposition, or background, but avoid anything that would offend him. By knowing what we face ahead of time, the inter- rogator can prepare himself for the general line of conversation he plans to pursue. A short man, a cripple, or an extremely tall man all have problems that are well to avoid in the interrogation room. I think that the best book on this subject that I have come across is *The Practical Psychology of Police Interrogation*, by Hugh C. McDonald.

Mr. McDonald has taken many physical propensities and described the possible psychological and personality results. His valuable book describes how to overcome some of these problems, and—of utmost importance—what to expect from some of the physical types when you first meet them. I would suggest that the above book be included in your study of the art of interrogation.

The next item to note on the pedigree sheet is the former address and/or the place of birth. What better conversation starter could be had than if you know something about the previous home town of the suspect. Immediately, you and he establish a contact or association that could produce very effective results later in the interrogation. If the suspect feels you are interested in him and are on his side, it will be a lot easier to convince him to come across with the information you seek. Even if you don't know anything about the place of birth or former residence, you haven't lost anything, and with a little asking around, you might find a few kind words to say about the place. Almost everyone is proud of his home town, and it never hurts to reinforce this feeling of understanding on your part by saying something kind about his place of birth, provided you know something about it. Never bluff on this point.

The subject's occupation will often indicate his aims and ideals, and it is well to note this fact. If the man is middle-aged and has been a laborer all of his life, it does no good to congratulate him on his successful business life because he knows as well as you do that he hasn't achieved financial success. However, if he has some skill or a professional position, then you can turn this to your advantage by congratulating him on his efforts and successes. If a man has thought enough of himself to make the effort to succeed in some skill, inherent in him is self-pride. Turn this to your advantage by letting him know that you also are proud of him, and that you'd be disappointed if he conducted himself other than as a successful man should. With more imagination on this point, you can discover for yourself other skills, trades, and occupations that will lend themselves to your use as an interrogator. Knowing in advance this fact about a suspect can help you arrange your thoughts and plans for the coming interrogation.

The subject's family, parents, brothers, sisters, and in-laws are always to be considered when talking to a suspect. There are several interrogation techniques that employ the suspect's family, and further reading about interrogation will teach you how to use these in your interrogation. My job here is not to teach the technique involved, but only to introduce you to some important factors to consider in this interrogation business so you'll know what to look for. If the subject has any family feeling at all, he will usually inject it sometime in your conversation with him. If you arm yourself with some few facts ahead of time, you can again impress him with your interest in him, and establish the contact with him that you will need to get a confession.

The subject's education is an all-important fact to note. If you find out his educational level prior to the interrogation, you are that much better off. If you don't know by the time the interrogation starts, find out as soon as you can and key your conversation accordingly. Talking to a suspect with words beyond his understanding will cause him to concentrate on your words rather than what you are saying. If you are talking below the level of the suspect, he, in turn, will consider you not too bright, and will not be inclined to place too much faith in you or your offers of friendship. Always try and use words that the suspect will understand so he can get the full meaning of your conversation. Do not try to impress him with your words, and never use words that you don't understand yourself. A relatively simple, concise vocabulary is far more effective than some ignorant drawl or some high-sounding speech that no one but yourself understands. Make the person know exactly what you are talking about in words and phrases that he can understand. A good example of not understanding words is the judge who asked, "Are you the defendant in this case?" The old hobo answered, "No, Suh, I've got a lawyer to do my defending. I'm the party what stole the chickens."

Avoid any discussion of religion unless you believe it's for the suspect's own good. Avoid particularly any denominational discussion of religion because you really open up a lot of prejudices in this area of conversation. You might mention the one religion the suspect is violently opposed to, and lose the whole trend of the conversation. It is best to avoid religion in your interrogation until you are well advanced in the art and know exactly how far to go, and especially, what not to say.

Now you have a pretty accurate description of the subject, his education, background, occupation, and many, many other facts that take him out of the unknown and equip you with a great deal of information. Some of the shadow of the unknown has been rolled back from the man or woman, and you can enter the interrogation with a feeling of knowledge and confidence. The best way to eliminate fear is through knowledge, and the better you prepare yourself prior to the interrogation, the more confident you will be. This confidence will be evident in your manner, and will tend to settle the suspect down if he sees that you are relaxed and at ease when you enter the interrogation room.

The next logical place to check for background information about the person that you intend to interrogate is your central records system. Most police departments have cabinets of old reports, usually kept for years. By going to these files and checking on your suspect, you can determine if he has had contact with your department before, if he has a history of troubles or other difficulties with the local police. Quite often, a good tip-off on what to expect about a man's attitude comes from checking his past contacts. If a man has had a series of marital troubles with the police involved, he will not be as receptive to your friendliness as a man who had had no contacts with the police. If this subject has been arrested for resisting arrest or disturbing the peace or other similar-type offenses, he probably has a built-in resentment of law and order, and more specifically, he probably resents the police because they represent the enforcement of regulations. It pays to check for this record of a suspect and then use the information. It does no good to know any of these things about a suspect unless you incorporate it in your interrogation. By knowing some information about the suspect's contacts with the police, you can intelligently proceed to tentatively preplan some usable interrogation procedure.

One of the most overlooked sources of information on a suspect is the traffic violation section. Many jokes have been told of how a man's personality changes when he gets into his automobile. I believe a man's driving habits do demonstrate his attitudes and represent some aspects of his personality. I have known men who outwardly appeared quite law abiding, but who, when it came to traffic violations, were not concerned as much with violating the law as they were with getting caught. Checking these traffic records gives you some insight into the man's attitudes and some idea of his willingness to obey the law. Usually, a long list of traffic violations indicates in the person a deep-seated disrespect for the law.

For interrogation purposes, this is important to know. An appeal to the man that he should confess because of his respect for law and order will fall on deaf ears. A good interrogator never overlooks any source of information about his suspect, and I sincerely believe that a knowledge of the person's driving habits will furnish you with a good bit of insight as to how this person operates in society. Quite often, hostility, aggression, recklessness, and other attributes are demonstrated by a person's driving habits.

Always check the criminal records on any suspect to whom you intend to talk. If the man has been in serious trouble before, he has probably been interrogated before. He will have preset ideas on how he probably will be treated; too often, he feels he will be tricked or "conned" into some impossible situation. Always be certain of one fact. You are not there to trap this man, but you are there for a sincere search for the truth of the matter. Quite often, a man who has been in a good deal of trouble with the police, particularly enough trouble to send him to prison, will know as much about interrogation as you do. He can usually spot any tricks or slips that you make, and he can always catch you in any lies should you be dumb enough to try any with him. The best way to overcome this type of man, I have found, is to be as dead honest with him as you can be. Do not try anything fancy with him, but keep it all as point-blank honest as you can. If he asks you something you don't know, tell him you don't know rather than try to bluff him. Most men who have been in a lot of trouble will try to take over the conversation, and will try to steer the interrogation to anything but what you want to talk about. By knowing in advance just how much trouble this suspect has been in, you can go into the interrogation room prepared for whatever might come up. Check these records and, most particularly, the FBI rap sheet. By knowing in advance the man's records, you can then reach a more logical analysis of his attitude toward you as an interrogator, and toward the law in general.

Always check the man's personal property, both for clues to the crime and also for clues to his personality. A man's wallet is a very good indicator of his community activities, his associates, his habits, his social connections and levels. Think of things in your own wallet if you doubt this fact. By checking the cards and papers in a man's wallet, you can usually tell his interests, jobs, fraternal associations, and a lot of other indicators of the suspect's ideals and opinions of himself in society. By knowing some of these things before you talk to him, you can often key your conversation around some of the information that you have found in the wallet. If a person thinks enough of cards or papers to carry them in his wallet, he usually thinks enough of what it represents to be proud of it. What better interrogation or conversation point could be had than something that the suspect is proud of? Usually the suspect will be more than willing to talk about something of this nature. Quite often, some evidence of the crime itself can be found in the person's personal property. I imagine that this is a result of some perverse psychological principle causing us to collect mementos or souvenirs of places we have been. Often, a person will keep something of a crime around to remind himself of how smart he is, or to help him relive the excitement of the moment. Always look through a man's personal property prior to talking to him, as it often can give you that certain tip that will be needed to bring out the confession.

Other people's ideas about the suspect can be determined by contacting friends, relatives, associates, and witnesses. All this information should arm you with a fairly good insight toward him. By this time, you should have firmly planted in your mind some sound opinions of the man, his ideas, ideals, occupation, mental possibilities, education, background, family, and records. By considering all the accrued information, you should be able to achieve some pretty thorough ideas of what to expect from this subject. By being forearmed with this knowledge of the person to be interrogated, you are in the position of being able to lead the conversation. This point is always important, as you must always maintain control of the conversation. Remember the definition of interview: "Conversation with a purpose." The interrogation situation is even more exacting, and you must constantly keep in mind the purpose of the interrogation. By being armed with knowledge of the suspect, you are in a far better position to guide the talk toward the end purpose than by walking into the situation without any prior knowledge of the subject.

The background checks we have discussed are primarily for adults. However, in dealing with juveniles, most of the same places can be checked for information, plus a few others that should be discussed at this time. A prime source of information concerning the child is his school. Quite often, the school will possess knowledge of the child, his family, friends, and school troubles that you could not find any other place. Most schools are conscientious enough to have checked into the background of their students, and quite often they can furnish you with information that can be used to understand the child and his problems even before you talk to him. Also, they will maintain a record of any minor troubles the child might have encountered in school. If the child is constantly in trouble in school, he is fighting the constricting coil of control and you will want to know this before you begin to talk. If the person has exhibited shyness or backwardness, again you will want to be armed with this information to help you set the tone of your interrogation. Always check the school of any juvenile you handle, for it gives you a definite advantage in the interrogation room. Always check the juvenile court to determine if the child has come in contact with them. Often, the child's counselor can give you the exact line of questioning to follow that has caused the child to talk in the past. If not, at least the child's records will show his attitudes and position in society. All of this information can be used in determining what to say to the child. If this child is a first-timer, without any previous trouble or contact with the authorities, usually a sympathetic approach will be the most effective. If there has been a lot of trouble in the child's past, he will not go for this offered sympathy but will probably respond better to a logical or more adult approach. Most teen-agers like to think of themselves as being older than their years, and if you appeal to them as being young adults, it will often cause them to respond in what they think would be an adult manner. It never hurts to flatter a child somewhat, but you must never degrade or make derisive remarks about the child, or his age, or his immaturity. Usually, a child's antisocial behavior is his method of striking out against what he considers unfair. Mature or not, it is still the child's effort to correct something, and we must respect these feelings if we intend to have him cooperate with us. Certainly, to embarrass or ridicule and further frustrate the child is no way to appeal to him to confess and cooperate. Never ridicule or make fun of any child, because you just reinforce his objectionable reactions to society.

If we have checked all of the places mentioned for the subject's background information, we should have now a fairly well-developed composite of the person that we intend to talk to. I cannot repeat too often that you must be armed with background information about the suspect if you intend to successfully interrogate him. Basically, the information can be used to start and keep the conversation going; more importantly, the information can be used to draw a mental picture in your mind of what to expect from this person, and subsequently what you must do to get the confession.

After you have gathered all available background information on the subject, then study the case report itself. In the case report you will find all the details of the crime, times, places, and so forth, that are available to the police. If any lengthy investigation has been conducted, this file may be rather involved, but still it is the sum total of all the information available to you concerning the crime. You must commit this information to memory, as this supports the cause of the interrogation. I have found that the best way to study one of these case files is to sort out everything and place it in chronological order. Then, as you read the reports, you can see the offense and the investigation being built as you read along.

There are some very important points to commit to memory as you proceed through your study of the case. In the interrogation room, you should never resort to use of the reports if you can possibly avoid it. It is not only distracting to the suspect and yourself, but it shows the suspect that you are not too well armed with the information about the case. He might get the feeling that he can lie to you, and you will not know the difference. Certain items concerning the offense that should always be memorized are given below.

1. Complainant's name or the business offended, and the address. Ordinarily, you will know the area in your own city, and if the subject drops something about the area or nearby businesses in his accounting of his activities, you will know that you are on the right trail. If you are talking to a suspect about some specific offense and are not armed with even the name and address of the offended, the suspect will be hard put to think that you are much interested in him, the case, or

for that matter, your job. Most confessions come because the suspect believes that you are honest and really sincerely interested in his welfare, and are suggesting what you think is the best thing for him to do. If you allow the suspect to see that you are just bluffing or are not really interested in either the case or him, you will not usually get the confession you are seeking.

2. Time and date of the offense. By knowing exactly when this offense occurred, you can direct your discussion and search for information concerning a specific area of time. Most suspects will start off by talking about everything but the time involved in the offense; however, if you know the exact time, you can constantly direct the conversation to cover the time the offense occurred. The time factor is important for you to know, as it gives you a guide toward which to aim the conversation.

3. Exactly what was taken if it was a robbery. Again, you must be prepared for any slips the suspect might make. If he does begin to confess, you must be able to lead him to the complete confession. It does no good to guess at stolen items, because if you suggest something that he did not take, he might think that you are trying to load him up and he may suddenly stop confessing. Commit to memory, in detail, all of the missing items so you can intelligently discuss not only the items but possibly the uses the suspect might make of the articles if, in fact, he did take them.

4. Method of operation in as much detail as is possible. In any conversation with a suspect, you must have a step-by-step accounting in your mind of the crime. You cannot talk at all about any offense if you do not know exactly, and in every detail, what happened. The only intelligent way to bring your suspect along is to fit your interrogation to exactly what happened step by step at the scene of the crime. Further, your conversation with the subject might still be at the "general" stage and you might not have begun to discuss the facts of the case with him. He might make some slip that will be the vital clue to prove he did what you suspect him of. I recall talking to a rather "hard" young man who, in the beginning, had told me that he wasn't about to say anything about anything. I started talking at random about trouble and the things a man should do, and finally told him that he should tell the truth about trouble. He answered,

"I'm not going to tell you about any breaks." I then asked him how he knew we were talking about a break and shortly, he confessed to it. This example points out that the interrogator must know all the elements of the crime; if the suspect makes a slip, be alert to it as it may be the key to a confession. The business of learning the exact "M.O." is also important when your subject begins to make his confession. Check him as he goes along to determine if he is telling you the complete truth. Also, use suggestive questions that will cause him to answer with information that only the perpetrator of the crime would know. Most M.O.'s will also give you some clue to the personality of the perpetrator. Mr. McDonald covers this field, and it is well to remember what you read on the subject. Often, some excellent clues are learned from the report as to what to expect from a guilty subject. Indiscriminate destruction, defecating on the floor, or excessive neatness at the scene of a crime will often lead you to a certain person as each person acts out his personality and its relationship to the world around him. He demonstrates this in crime; thus, often by learning all of the facts about a crime, you can see some of the suspect's attitudes toward life in his actions at a crime scene. The time element and the crime scene M.O. must be tied together in your mind and in your conversation. As you talk to a suspect and are having him account for his time, these two factors become very important. Suppose he is stating that it took thirty minutes to go from A to C Street, and the offense is that someone broke a jewelry store window, grabbed a watch, and ran. You know that A and C Streets are only two blocks apart, and you immediately have him in a position of having to explain the time factor much closer than he would have if you had not been alert. Always get every detail of the crime as you study the case file.

5. Witnesses and their observations of what they saw. As you talk to your suspect, you should stop him occasionally and ask him who he saw or who saw him as he relates his story of his activities. If you know from the witnesses the times and places they saw the suspect, you can often spot the point where the suspect is straying from the truth as he talks to you. Further, you can also support a witness' testimony if the suspect in his account verifies that he saw the witness. By correlating the facts of the crime with the witnesses' testimony,

you can usually decide in your mind how the crime was committed. Then, as you talk to your suspect, you can guide his conversation along the lines that you know it must take.

6. Evidence. Always check all of the evidence involved in any case. Pay particular attention to any peculiar markings or identification marks on any evidence. As you talk along or even as you begin to get the confession, you will want to check the suspect by allowing him to describe just what he saw or describe the item he saw. By knowing exactly what an item looks like yourself, you will be in a position of knowing, for a fact, if he is telling the whole truth. Always check and determine if any physical evidence of the criminal himself was obtained. Things such as fingerprints, footprints, and personal items dropped are real wedges in the interrogation technique. I never feel that it is a good idea to rush in and say "OK, give up, we have your fingerprints." You probably will have to prove the case in court if you do, because by scaring a suspect you make him further hide behind his story. But if you are armed with these physical facts, you can inject them into your conversation as you go along, building up the logical wall of truth and showing the suspect that he might as well confess. Always do it the easy way. Even a suspect in the most vicious crime is a human being and entitled to the human dignities that we all expect and need. If you treat every suspect with respect, your results will be more continuously effective. Being armed with all the facts of a case, which includes knowing all the evidence in the case, places you in a much better position to discuss the offense in detail with the suspect. I personally am always very leary about bluffing (indicating that I have some physical evidence in a case that I don't actually have). I would say that as a general practice, it is bad business. If your suspect is guilty as charged but knows that he wore gloves the whole time he was in a building, and you sit there and tell him you have fingerprints from the safe, he will immediately know that you are lying to him. If you lie to him, and he catches you at it, you might as well get up and leave, for the suspect will have no more faith in you or what you say to him. I have heard it said that you can bluff if you make sure you don't get caught, but I would suggest to a beginning interrogator that he should never bluff, because he will get caught. It takes a

real expert to successfully bluff, and there just aren't too many of them around.

As you can see, we should now have a fairly well-developed picture of both the offense itself and the suspect if we have checked all of the available sources of information and have actually learned and thought about this information. To recap the foregoing information, I am going to list here the sources that we have just read about. I feel that this list should be made a part of your mental check-off list. If you avail yourself of this information every time that you are going to interrogate a suspect, you will find that your success level will be greatly enhanced.

Suspect Information
1. Mugging and printing information.
2. Central records information.
3. Traffic records information.
4. Criminal records information.
5. Personal property information.
6. School information (juvenile).
7. Juvenile court (juvenile).

Case Information
1. Information request sheet.
2. Case file.
3. Evidence.
4. Interview with investigators.
5. Interview with witnesses.

Chapter 3

SELF-PREPAREDNESS

Now that you have equipped yourself with all the available information concerning the suspect, the next job is to get yourself prepared mentally for the job to be done. Proper mental preparation for the coming interrogation is as important as having all of the facts available. Being mentally prepared is one thing, but don't be like the fellow who was asked, "Did anyone ever tell you how wonderful you are?" He replied, "No, I don't think anyone ever did." The questioner replied, "Then I'd like to know how you got the idea!"

Being self-prepared is best summed up by the phrase, "Believe in yourself." It is easy for me to tell you to believe in yourself. Where do you start? How do you develop this self-confidence in the interrogation practice? First, we have already studied one aspect of self-preparedness as we read about the case and the subject. Certainly, by knowing things about the subject and all about the case, we have insured ourselves against the fear of meeting the unknown. This part of the book will cover other points to be considered in our interrogation preparation. To be totally prepared for an interrogation is no small task. Most of what we study here is a constant effort with us and is, therefore, not something that we must undergo just prior to each interrogation. Considering these next suggestions of self-preparation will make each of us a better interrogator.

Let us start first with some interpersonal problems that should be considered before starting this interrogation business. By some introspection before we start our interrogation work, we can come to grips with some important personal facts that must be resolved to become good at our job. I realize that we all will not reach the same decision as to what to do about these problems, but recognizing some of the problems beforehand better prepares us to become good interrogators because we will better know ourselves. When we contact another person, we must concede that some of our personality shows through. As interrogators, we will want to eliminate as much of our offensive behavior as we possibly can. We cannot do the job of interrogation if, on the first contact, the suspect takes objection to us. By looking at ourselves first and considering some items that can be improved about ourselves, we remove some roadblocks and make it eaiser for a suspect to confess to us. By looking at ourselves and resolving to change, eliminate, or improve certain personality traits, we do yet another thing to help us "believe in ourselves": we prepare our personality for the job of interrogation. I do not imply that you'll have to remake your personality; I only suggest some points for consideration that should make you a better interrogator.

As important as any single item in this examination is *self-respect*. Of course, everything that we have done or have been exposed to in our development has helped form our self-respect. If we don't have respect for ourselves, in all probability we will not respect others. By the same token, if we respect ourselves and conduct ourselves in a manner that deserves respect, most people will afford us the respect we deserve. In our contact with a suspect, if we respect ourselves and in turn, afford the suspect the respect that he deserves, we make a much better impression than when we deride or embarrass him. Self-respect is not something you can ask for or buy; it is something you earn by your own actions. If you always consider your actions and conduct yourself in a prudent and intelligent manner, it will be evident to all you come in contact with, including the suspect. Remember that the suspect is a human being and will respond much easier if you treat him as such without resorting to indignities. Dignity and self-respect are something that shines from within, and you can only achieve this inner glow if you conduct yourself in such a manner as to warrant it.

A problem with all of us will be *temper*. I have never seen a confession obtained by an interrogator who lost his temper. In fact, if you do lose your temper, you might as well quit for you have lost control of the situation. Temper is something that you must learn to leave outside the interrogation room regardless of the type of case that you must handle. Many suspects, particularly those who have been in trouble before, will attempt to upset the interrogator. This is how they defend themselves and avoid talking about the case in which they are a suspect. Temper is one luxury you cannot afford to have when you are dealing with a man's freedom. If what happened did not directly involve you, you cannot afford to become so personally involved as to lose your temper. Your job is to talk to the suspect, not to take sides or argue issues with him. If you can't control your temper as you talk, you will probably not make a good interrogator. Only if you act calm and self-assured will the suspect respect you. Remember, when you have a person in custody, he knows that he's a suspect and he's already upset, frightened, and ready to defend himself in any way he can. If you lose your temper, all you do is add to the confusion and completely eliminate the possibility of calming this person down enough so he will confess. Temper can and must be controlled if you intend to be a successful interrogator. Develop the habit of taking a "disinterested interest" in the situation, and you'll be far better able to control your temper. "Patience is a virtue" is the saying, and it's a virtue that a good interrogator must have.

An integral part of a person's exhibited personality is his *integrity*. The dictionary describes integrity as being "a soundness of moral character; uprightness." It is well to remember that as you sit in the interrogating room and reach decisions about the suspect he, in turn, is doing the same thing. It becomes apparent all too quickly when a person does not appear whole and complete in his reactions to another. Just by expressions and word shadings, a person can suggest the fact that he's not as trustworthy as he might be. As you sit in the interrogation room, you want to radiate the fact that you are a sincere, upright individual. Because of this and what you say to the suspect, he can assume that you are sincere and honest. If you appear to be the kind of person who is on the right track in life, the suspect can look up to you. You can rest assured that if this suspect does not have respect for you, he will not confess to you. Integrity is not something that you can put on or off like a coat, but must be a part of everything you do each day. If we get in the habit of doing everything in an honest and forthright manner, we will soon exhibit this soundness of moral character by our conscious and subconscious acts. If we are slick and evasive in our actions, this too shows through and will prevent us from doing any job effectively.

The matter of a person's *vocabulary* is a rather delicate thing to discuss, but is an absolute necessity in considering an interrogator. Usually, vocabulary is a matter of choice with the individual. Most of us stop reading and learning when we leave school, and this is extremely unfortunate. I do not advocate the use of high-sounding words, but I do say that a good interrogator must know the meanings of more than a few "big" words. It is extremely uncomfortable to be sitting in an interrogation room with a suspect who has a more than average education, and not know exactly what he is talking about. If the suspect is suspicious of this fact, he can completely take the offensive away from you, and you lose the whole interrogation when he does. Mr. Herbert V. Prochnow in his book, *The Successful Speaker's Handbook*, has this to say about vocabulary:

> The words that will express your ideas in conversation are the same words that you should use on your feet. Simplicity of expression makes for ease in understanding. The simpler you can make the talk—that is— in the words you use, the more assurance you have that everyone in your audience will be able to follow you. You will know that the least edu- cated will understand what you are saying, and you cannot offend the most educated, because he, too, will know what you mean and will have your idea vividly impressed upon his mind.

The proper use of words is far more important than the use of "big" words. In the interrogation room, you are not attempting to impress the person with how intelligent you are, but you are trying to reach him with some common-sense ideas that he can understand and use to decide that what you suggest is the right thing to do. He can reach no decision if he doesn't understand you. Consider every idea that you intend to suggest as an artist would consider a landscape, you use words to paint the verbal picture that you want to create in the suspect's mind. Don't forget any of the details in your verbal picture, and you will see the suspect begin to see the suggestions take shape as you make them, just as the artist's picture becomes clearer as he works on it. It does no harm to limit your interrogation vocabulary to the more common words if you use them well and colorfully. You must, however, know some of the more commonly used "big" words or you will be at a loss sometimes. Never resort to slovenly pronounced or drawl-type conversation. The uneducated suspect is fully aware of his own limitations, and will probably assume that you are making fun of his efforts rather than consider you as one of the boys. Use of professional slang should be limited also, as most people do not know what it means. If you use the slang of the subject, do not go overboard with it. He knows that you are not part of his crowd or group, and will begin to suspect that you are only attempting to ingratiate yourself. Never use slang words that you don't understand, and if you do use the suspect's slang, make it sound sincere and as if you occasionally used the word yourself. Never make the suspect's slang sound like a funny word when you say it. Never, never use words that you do not understand yourself. The suspect might know exactly what it means, and you can turn a serious conversation into a joke by the use of a wrong word. Think about what you say before you say it, and you will usually stay out of trouble. Psychologically, a person can think at about 400 words a minute, and he can speak at about 125 words a minute. The suspect is hearing everything you say, thinking it out, and planning what he intends to say in return as you talk. Don't give him any fuel by improperly using words. Common words, artfully used, will afford you the most success.

Much consideration should be given to your own individual *prejudices*. Right now, racial problems are much in the news. Prejudices, however, do not stop at just how we feel about the different races. Social position, certain types of crimes, moral affairs, and so on, can all be mixed up within each of us so that we will take a prejudiced attitude toward them. It is my opinion that a law enforcement officer cannot afford to be prejudiced. This, I know, is a broad statement and is practically impossible to abide by. The next best thing, then, is for the officer to leave his prejudiced opinions at home, or at the very least, outside the interrogation room. Immediately apparent are a person's prejudices if he makes no attempt to control them. If you have to come into contact with some situation or person that you consider inferior, you will make your feelings very apparent if you are not careful. You will have no effect at all on this person if you enter into the conversation with a closed mind and preconceived ideas. If you are violently opposed to some proposition, and you know it in advance, don't enter an interrogation room, because you will hurt someone else's chances. As an interrogator, you are not the judge, and you do not have the right to judge the person right or wrong in society's eyes. It takes effort on your part to make some suspects believe that you are an open-minded, fair person, but if you can do it, you will succeed where narrow-minded, prejudiced people fail. The mark of a good interrogator is that he will be able to talk to all people, regardless of race, religion, or type of crime with the same calm sincerity and warmness. Prejudice has no place in a good interrogator, and actually has no place in an intelligent man. If you are going to be good at your job, it might take some soul searching, but you will be a better human being and a better interrogator for it.

I have been in interrogation rooms and heard officers use degrading terms, both about themselves and about others. It is my opinion that *profanity* falls within this area of degrading oneself. An interrogator should never involve himself in any kind of degrading behavior and least of all behavior degrading to himself. This whole concept of interrogation is built on the concept of presenting yourself in such a light as to suggest trust. If you begin to build up this picture of being trustworthy, and then turn around and conduct yourself in some degrading manner, you will end up with a sum total of zero. Most people use some profanity, but you as an interrogator cannot afford to while you are talking to your suspect. If you, yourself, are seeking out advice or information from someone, you would be somewhat put out if this person used profanity or other disparaging conversation in his answer to you. You would not put much credit to what that person had to say and would not respect the person as much. The suspect is in the same position, seeking and needing advice, and he will not trust you or believe you as much as he would if you conducted yourself in a self-respecting, intelligent manner.

Another point to be remembered is to never put yourself in such a position that you need to defend yourself or your associates. Often, suspects will begin to run down the department or law enforcement in general. Never get involved in these discussions because, if you are completely honest, there are certain criticisms of any department that are warranted. If you conduct yourself in a manner that cannot be criticized, then you will not have to defend your actions, and will not come within the general framework of criticism in the suspect's mind. Remember that your purpose in the interrogation room is to get the confession, and you should do everything you can, including presenting yourself favorably, to get this confession. By not degrading yourself, you remove one point of conflict with the suspect, and you add to your chances for the confession by favorably presenting yourself.

All of you have met people in business who impressed you right away. Most sales schools teach that the first thirty seconds make the impression that makes the sale. Since we are trying to sell ourselves in the interrogation room, it is well to consider our impression on the suspect. When we meet professional people, we are usually impressed because of their businesslike, serious pride in their business. This serious, *professional attitude* is one that we, as interrogators, should adopt as our own. I know that a fun guy is a lot nicer to be around socially than a serious, solemn man, but in our professional activities, we prefer to be with a serious, businesslike person when we have a problem to solve. You have to be the judge of how to conduct yourself in the interrogation room, but a serious attitude should always be the one you start off with. The suspect is fully conscious of the fact that he is in trouble and will appreciate your taking a serious attitude rather than a lighthearted approach. Oftentimes during an interrogation, a situation will present itself where the subject appears to be funny or to have done something funny. Never take advantage of your position and laugh at him, because no one likes to be laughed at. Take your cue from the suspect, and if he laughs at himself then you can laugh; never originate the humor. I don't say that you must conduct yourself as if you possessed the wisdom of Solomon, but I do say that you should keep a serious attitude about the problems that are serious to the suspect.

In conjunction with this problem of seriousness is that you must never allow yourself to become bored. *Boredom* is all too evident, and if the suspect believes that you are bored with the whole conversation, he will not be as inclined to cooperate with you. Maintain an attentive attitude toward all that goes on in the interrogation room and you will impress him with your interest and desire to understand him. All of us are prone to allow our minds to wander onto other ideas, but this is something that we must fight against. Again, the problem is serious to the suspect, and if he catches you thinking about something else, he will know that you are not too interested in what he is saying or trying to explain. If you allow yourself to become bored, this in turn makes you somewhat mentally dull, and you can never compete with this person if you are not thinking about the case at hand. The problems of seriousness and boredom are something that you must make up your mind to even before you enter the interrogation room. Both have a direct relation to the impression that you are going to make on the suspect. A good impression is what you want and need if you intend to get the confession.

Most people, interrogators included, are too prone to enjoy the sound of their own voices. I have heard that the sweetest sound in the world is your own name, and the second is the sound of your own voice. All of us are convinced that what we have to say is probably the best advice in the world, and anyone who doesn't agree just isn't with it. In the interrogation room, this feeling can be a real drawback. Our job is to get the confession, and not to hear ourselves speaking. I heard one prisoner try to break into the conversation of an interrogator for the express purpose of confession. The interrogator was so immersed in the sound of his own voice and words that it took some effort on the part of the suspect to confess. This case is unusual, but the fact that the interrogator overtalked is not unusual. In another case, my opening words to a suspect were "Do you know why you are here?" He answered "Sure, it's because I had intercourse with my daughter." I asked him why he hadn't told the others about the offense, and he replied that no one had come right out and asked him. All the other words used by the other interrogators had been wasted, when all they had to do was let the suspect talk. This business of hearing one's own voice works for the suspect also. He likes to hear himself talk. That is what you want him to do if he will. You should say just enough to get him started and then shut up. A good listener is hard to come by and also is difficult to be, but it is necessary if you intend to become a good interrogator. Interrogation is not all talking; it is part listening and allowing the suspect to talk. Often, as he talks, he will come right out with the admission that you are seeking.

All of us have certain *nervous habits* that, in the field of interrogation, we must become aware of. In an interrogation room, the interrogator must train himself to sit perfectly still and let only his voice move the person. Hand twitching, foot shuffling, fingernail cleaning, and any other movement will be distracting to the suspect, and can cause his attentiveness to your words to be lost. Any movements that you make will be noticed by the suspect, and you must exclude them from your conduct in the interrogation room. Nothing is more distracting than some nervous habit, particularly if it is repeated over and over. You, as the interrogator, must not be guilty of these nervous habits as you must not give the suspect anything else to think about other than your words. It requires a lot of patience to sit perfectly still for a long period of time, but you must develop this habit. This is also very important if there is another interrogator in the room and you are sitting, listening. Never do anything that would attract attention to yourself and distract from the other interrogator's words. A still, quiet, relaxed attitude will put the suspect's attention on your words, not on your nervousness. Further, your nervousness will tend to increase the suspect's nervousness, and will tip him off to the fact that you are not quite sure of yourself. Interrogation requires that you calm the suspect down, remove his fears, and obtain the confession. Your nervous habits have an opposite effect, and you must try to control them.

To succeed in the interrogation room, you must *become impersonally involved* in the interrogation. It must be an absolutely controlled involvement, but you must make the involvement appear sincere and heartfelt. Involvement includes this business of seriousness, interest, attention, and also a good bit of acting. If the suspect wants to cry, make it appear that you want to cry with him. If he wants an ultra-sincere conversation, you must appear to be almost conspiring with him. This involvement will mean a good bit of acting on your part. You must overcome any shyness or embarrassment, and act out the part that you are trying to portray.

You must even put the right emphasis on your words to make them sound sincere and meaningful. To convince the suspect that you really understand his problem, you must play the part. This will take some practice. I have always felt that a good "con" man would probably make a very good interrogator. The ability to convince other people that you are what you say you are, and you mean every word that you speak, takes some practice and know-how. Eliminate your own natural shyness from your interrogation attitude, and you will be able to put across any idea that you want. Above all, in all your acting, you must make it as believable as you can. Being a little extroverted is in no way harmful in becoming a good interrogator. You must be what the suspect needs at the time, and you will get the confession. You must be involved in the interrogation, but again, in a completely controlled attitude. You must make the suspect believe that you are really interested in every word he says, and are completely sincere in your reactions to his words. Complete interest, attentive listening, straightforward conversation, sitting still, and apparent emotional involvement will convince the suspect that you are interested in him and his story and will convince him that you are the person that he should confess to. You must appear to be sincere or you will look foolish to the suspect, and you will lose him if he feels that you are only putting on an act. It requires practice to portray this "face of involvement," but you will gain many more confessions than if you omitted this aspect of your interrogative development.

Finally, you must learn to be *impartial*. This, in itself, is no small problem to most of us. I have told you to learn the case and try to draw some logical conclusion as to how the offense happened. I have told you to keep the purpose of the interrogation in mind, and to strive for the confession from your suspect. But you must remember that the person that you are talking to might *not* be guilty. Never back yourself into a corner in the interrogation room by accusing the suspect until he admits he is the guilty party or has given you some reason to believe that he is the guilty party. As the opening line in the chapter states, one person's words are not enough; you must get both sides to form a conclusion. It might be in some case that the complainant has not been completely honest with the investigators—

suspect is involved in something, but is not the actual guilty party. Maintain an impartial attitude throughout the interrogation, and you will not be put in the position of having to make excuses. After all, the courts try the person; you are only an investigator for the court, not the person who has to make the decision of guilt or innocence. By remaining impartial, you can also keep yourself on the sidelines, so to speak, and be in a better position to analyze the suspect's reactions, your words and actions, and the facts of the case. You cannot think straight if you prejudge the person or if you become so personally involved in the case that you develop likes and dislikes. I have seen interrogators personally involved with a suspect, and they usually become very sensitive to the suspect and all that he says. This personal sensitivity often leads to harsh words and useless conversations with the suspect. Personal involvement with the suspect is useless, inept, and without justifiable excuse on the part of the officer. If the involvement is a controlled act, OK, but if it becomes a personality contest, then it is wrong. Harsh words or disagreements between you and the suspect seldom lead to confessions.

To sum up this chapter of the book briefly, all of the foregoing suggestions have been pointed toward a more profound "belief in yourself." I do not believe in too much self-analysis, because most of us are not trained well enough to come up with adequate answers for all of our personal problems. However, I do believe that by considering and controlling some of the outward exhibitions of our personality, we can become more effective interrogators. I do not think that just "a way with words" is enough to be a good interrogator. A multitude of other factors are involved, and all should receive equal consideration and thought. The personality factors that we just examined are but a few items in our total dynamic makeup. I do not have the space in this kind of book to discuss every facet of the personality that will be involved in an interrogation, but I do feel that the foregoing discussion will serve to point out the idea that I am trying to get across. A good interrogator must be in control of himself, and know that he is adequately prepared for the forthcoming interrogation. If he believes in himself, he will have looked at his own personality and eliminated, or at least tried to control, those aspects of himself that might be offensive to others. You do not want the suspect to think of you as a person, but you do want him to think of you as an idea. The presentation of this idea will involve your personality, and you want everything controlled and presented to the suspect so you know he will receive the idea that you are trying to put across. If you can control your own personality to the degree that you are allowing the suspect to see only the idea that you are presenting (that it is best for him to confess to you), then you have accomplished what every interrogator sets out to do. By being in complete control of yourself, you will remain in control of the interrogation situation. Through necessity, this control involves making your personality as acceptable to the suspect as is possible.

Chapter 4

SOME DO'S AND DON'TS

I NEVER LIKE to include a list of do's and don'ts in an effort such as this, but if you will think of them as just a list of suggestions to consider while you are in the interrogation room itself, I feel that you will benefit. Every interrogation will differ somewhat, and you will have to fit yourself to the situation. However, certain suggestions will remain constant. You must learn to keep your mind alert and active to the changing situations that occur as you talk to your suspect. What I am offering here are a few suggestions that will fit almost every occasion. The one thing about a good interrogator is that he will remain alert to every changing action and mood. Much the same way, I imagine, as the ninety-year-old man who was asked how he maintained his good health. His answer was, "Well, Captain, when I works, I works hard; but when I sits, I sits loose." A good interrogator must learn to sit loose, and be alert to every changing aspect of the interrogation situation. He can do this if he has introduced in himself an attitude that will cause him to do the right things automatically, and not do the wrong things thoughtlessly. The only way that you will become good at interrogation is through practice, but you must know a few things that it pays to do, and a few more that it never pays to do. So, my following list of do's and don'ts. These are suggestions that I have found to work for me, and I feel that if you will include them in your bag of tricks, you will find that they will work for you too. You will notice that, following this list, I have included a discussion of why they have been suggested. I feel that anyone trying to pass along information should be able to justify his recommendations. This business of learning is hard enough without having to accept someone's unsupported ideas. Trying to teach has its drawbacks also, much like the little boy felt when his mother asked him, "Well, dear, what did Mama's little baby learn in school

[35]

today?" And the reply, "I learnt two kids not to call me Mama's little baby!"

I believe that if you remember the do's and don'ts in these lists, you will have far more success inside the interrogation room. These facts, coupled with what we have already discussed, will tend to make you a far more successful interrogator.

Do	Don't
1. Do be organized in your thinking and talking.	1. Don't discourage the suspect.
2. Do be businesslike.	2. Don't antagonize or patronize.
3. Do make a good impression.	3. Don't pencil-listen.
4. Do keep relating the conversation to the purpose of interrogation.	4. Don't ever act surprised at an admission.
5. Do avoid cockiness.	5. Don't condemn.
6. Do avoid preconceived ideas.	6. Don't appear to dominate.
7. Do avoid outside pressures.	7. Don't be impressed by subject's social or economic position.
8. Do avoid display of police power.	
9. Do avoid use of realistic words such as kill, shoot, rape.	8. Don't ever make any promises.
10. Do sit close.	9. Don't ever threaten.
11. Do minimize smoking.	10. Don't ever use coercion.
12. Do avoid shackles.	11. Don't be guilty of duress.
13. Do keep upper hand.	12. Don't ever strike or manhandle a suspect.
14. Do take proper amount of time.	13. Don't deny him the human comforts to which he is entitled.
15. Do keep subject at ease; protect him from embarrassment.	
16. Do know human behavior.	14. Don't deny him his rights as provided by law.
17. Do *know the law*.	

I realize that this is a rather lengthy list; however, I feel as you review it, you will notice that most of these suggestions are just common-sense ideas. If you always remember that every suspect is a human being with the same kind of feelings you have, you will find that the application of these suggestions is almost automatic. Nothing disgusts me more than to see a prisoner abused. I feel that it puts the abuser on the bottom of the pile. This whole book has been written so that you can succeed with your mind and voice, and never stoop to physical violence.

In discussing each of the foregoing suggestions, I will take each list separately and note the item as it appears on the list, with a discussion of it immediately below.

DO

The do's are explained below.

1. Do be organized in your thinking. When I mention the word organized, I do not mean regimented or single-minded to the degree that you cannot accept a changing situation. By this suggestion, I mean you should have all of the facts at your fingertips, and have them organized well enough in your mind so you can proceed through an interrogation without having to resort to notes or reports. Know the crime and its elements, know the subject and his background to the best of your ability, and know the basic elements of interrogation to a degree that you can successfully use them without constantly having to stop and think. If you are organized when you begin your interrogation, the conversation will flow easily without abrupt and unnecessary pauses. An interrogator will attempt to keep the conversation flowing in an easy, effortless manner. If he has organized all of the facts that he has to deal with, he can accomplish this easygoing manner. If he is half-prepared and disorganized in his thinking, it will certainly show in his efforts. Interrogation is an art, and the better prepared you are, the easier it will be to convince the suspect that he should tell you the truth.

2. Do be businesslike. The old saying that you can erase every impression except the first one is certainly true. If you conduct yourself in a businesslike, professional manner you cannot fail to make a good first impression. Do not try and rush the suspect off his feet, but do start all of your interrogations in a matter-of-fact, businesslike manner. If you create the impression of being confident that you will get the truth from the suspect, you can often convince him that

it will do him no good to lie to you. We have discussed a professional, businesslike attitude previously. If you enter the interrogation room confident that you will get what you are after, and let your voice and actions reflect this confidence, you will automatically assume a businesslike demeanor. Make it appear that you would be shocked if the suspect told you anything but the truth. Often, this act alone will be enough to bring out the truth.

3. Do make a good impression. Again, this suggestion of good impression. All of the list of things for you to do should bring about a good impression. The reason the idea is singled out is only to bring it into clear focus. You have only yourself and your words to sell, and you must do the best with them that you can. There is nothing about you that would make a person confess, except that something which you teach yourself to have. You must know how to say the words, how to act as you talk, and what words to say. In other words, you want to impress on the person with whom you are talking the fact that you are the man to whom he should confess. Only by making a good impression on the suspect will this confession happen. Everything that you do and say will go into making your impression on him, and you, therefore, will want to do everything right. Keeping in mind that you want to favorably impress your suspect with your ideas will help toward the end result of a confession.

4. Do keep relating the conversation to the purpose of the interrogation. A suspect will usually, particularly if he is being evasive, attempt to talk about everything except what you are after. You must be ever attentive to the trend of the conversation, and adroitly keep steering it back on course. If you remain on top of the situation, you can tell when your subject begins to drift or make long winded explanations about irrelevant matters, and you can inject a few words, or maybe a question, that will get the subject back on track. Most subjects will go into lengthy explanations of some kind, usually about all the little events that happened before or after the crime. They do this to avoid reaching the point where they have to talk about the incident itself. Some will lightly skip over the incident, and proceed to other subjects. You must then retract slightly, and get the full details of the incident. Never let a suspect outtalk you in a rambling manner. Interrupt and get the story back into focus

before either of you becomes too tired, or the interrogation gets over-long. It never hurts to let a suspect explain, but you must guide the conversation constantly toward the purpose of the interrogation.

5. Do avoid cockiness. A wise-guy attitude never works for an interrogator, and is usually done to cover up an unsureness on his part. You do not need to be a cocky wise guy if you know your business and are sure of what you are doing. Cockiness usually denotes immaturity, and certainly has no part in a professional interrogator.

6. Do avoid preconceived ideas. Don't be like the accused man who was asked by the prosecutor, "Now tell the court how you came to take the car." The accused answered, "Well, the car was parked in front of the cemetery, so naturally I thought the owner was dead." You can look just as silly if you go into an interrogation with your mind already made up. As an interrogator, you are searching for the truth, and you cannot know what the truth is until after you talk to your suspect. Take an objective approach that is free from personal feelings and prejudices. Let the sum result of your inter-rogation help you make up your mind; don't rely just on the one side you have heard before talking to the suspect.

7. Do avoid outside pressures. Don't ever let someone else talk you into believing anything about the suspect until you find it out for yourself. Some officer may say you cannot break this subject as he is too hard. If you believe him, you probably can't break him. If the crime is a serious one and the offended is someone of influence, never let this fact enter the interrogation room with you. If your suspect is guilty, you try for the confession, but if he is innocent, you want to prove that also. Whatever anyone tells you about a suspect should be considered as *his* opinion; never accept it as your own opinion until you have proven it for yourself. Never let someone else's opinion influence your own, because he might be wrong. After you have interrogated and reached an opinion, stand by it and don't let outside pressures change you, unless they can prove you absolutely wrong.

8. Do avoid display of police power. Needless to say, any kind of weapon, badge, nightstick or other paraphernalia in the sight of an accused can be construed to be a threat. It's impossible to defend their exposure in court, so they should be eliminated before you go

into an interrogation situation. A detective or plainclothesman should always wear a coat to cover any of his equipment, and a uniformed officer should remove his badge, hat, gunbelt, cuffs, and blackjack or nightstick before entering into an interrogation room. If there has been too much of a display of equipment, and the subject changes his mind in court about how you got the confession, you can be made to look like a real brute. We will talk about the place to interrogate later in the book, but you should always remember that you should avoid anything that smacks of police power or the police station during your interrogation.

9. Do avoid use of realistic words such as kill, shoot, steal. In our English language, there are certain words that are shocking, particularly when applied to the field of crime. When you are interrogating a person, you should avoid the use of these realistic words, as it only serves to upset a person when he is constantly reminded of the seriousness of the offense. Employ euphemisms. Rather than "shoot," you could say "fire a gun." Instead of "kill," you could use "died"; rather than "steal," you could use "took or carried off." At this stage in the interrogation, it all means the same, but it does not sound the same. The facts make up a crime and it doesn't really make any difference what you call it. One technique is that of reducing the seriousness of the crime, and I feel that it is well to consider this point in your use of the words to describe the act. To use a less harsh-sounding word does not reduce your ability to discuss the crime, but it does reduce the serious "sounds" of the crime in the mind of the suspect. No one likes to admit any mistake, and the bigger the mistake, the tougher it is to admit. By softening the words somewhat, you make it just a little easier for the person to confess. If you consider all of the words connected with the particular crime you are discussing and try and reduce the harsh implications they carry, you will settle the suspect down faster and get the confession sooner.

10. Do sit close. If you sit directly in front of the suspect and remove any tables or chairs from in between, you will have eliminated any support the suspect may derive from their presence. If there is a table between you and the suspect, he can lean on it and get support, and he can also achieve a certain sense of satisfaction from

the fact that it is a barrier between you and him. A table serves to prop up both the interrogator and the suspect, and should be eliminated. By sitting close, you can talk lower and more intimately, and you can hear everything the suspect says and see everything that he does.

11. Do minimize smoking. A great deal of nervous tension is aleviated by the act of smoking, and most of us smoke to reduce nervousness and cover any uncertainties we might feel. If we spend an hour building the suspect to the point where he is about to reach the decision to confess and then offer him a smoke, we might lose him. The act of smoking will give him time to think and reduce the tension level we have created; he might decide not to confess. Smoking also gives a person something to do with his hands and mouth, and something to think about. If we are trying to create the feeling in the suspect that he should confess, smoking will do nothing but distract from our effort. However, if you do have to smoke in the interrogation room, every time you have a cigarette, offer the suspect one. It not only is the decent thing to do, but will show him that you are not against him, and are only trying to help.

12. Do avoid shackles. Not much will be said about this point. It is absolutely wrong to interrogate someone in shackles. I do not feel that I need to justify this point, as I hope the day of this kind of treatment is dead and buried, along with the bright lights and rubber hoses.

13. Do keep the upper hand. The ability to control an interrogation will grow with each succeeding interrogation, but right from the start, you must make every effort to keep the upper hand in your conversation with the suspect. A calm, relaxed, businesslike attitude has covered many a faint heart in this kind of situation, and you must make it appear as if you had interrogated all of your life. By keeping your hands still and folded, you will not shake; by sitting still, you will not show your nervousness, and by using the words you are familiar with and knowing the case in advance, you can keep the tremor from your voice. Some suspects will attempt to bluff you with loud and boisterous talk, but you must never let them take over the conversation. Often, speaking a little softer than they will make them pause to hear what you have to say, and you can

make the point that their attitude is getting them nowhere. Always keep control of an interrogation.

14. Do take proper amount of time. You must put forth the idea that you have all the time in the world to talk with the suspect. If the suspect thinks that you have only a limited time to talk with him, he knows that all he has to do is hold out, and then you will let him alone. Never try to interrogate while you are involved in some other effort. Once you start the interrogation, you should stay with it and not be running in and out of the room trying to do a dozen other things. Every time you leave a suspect you break the chain of thought, and you will never succeed in bringing him around if you cannot keep him thinking of the offense. An old saying is that when you are all through with the interrogation and convinced you are getting nowhere, try one more time. Always take plenty of time to interrogate; don't try to accomplish everything at once. You are competing with a suspect for a confession that can mean months or years to him, and you can well afford to give him whatever time it takes to see justice done.

15. Do keep the subject at ease—protect him from embarrassment. I have seen officers, not involved in a case, make fun of some arrested person through their own ignorance. Certainly, nothing makes a person more defensive than someone laughing at him. This point is all too true in the case of juveniles. Never laugh at or make fun of a youngster, as this will do nothing but drive him further into his shell. If some outsider begins to kid your suspect, either move him away or ask the person to stop talking to him. You might make the kidder sore, but you avoid having him put your suspect in the frame of mind that will deny you the confession. The entire interrogation attitude is up to you, and you cannot afford to let someone else set the tone or ruin something that you have started. If you are attempting to be friendly and helpful with the suspect and show him you are on his side, someone making fun of him can ruin the whole atmosphere of understanding and interest. Try to keep yourself and your suspect out of any situation where outsiders can ruin your interrogation chances or techniques.

16. Do know human behavior. I do not suggest that you must

be a psychologist to be a good interrogator, but to be acquainted with some basic psychological principals will be of definite advantage. Just as the truth is logical and fits together like a jigsaw puzzle, human behavior must also be logical. As you talk to your suspect, always consider first of all whether what he says is physically possible; next, decide whether or not it seems to fit the pattern of the suspect's abilities and conduct. Do not be hard, cold, and rigid-minded on this idea, but do be alert to any conduct of your suspect that would be unusual to him and to his behavioral pattern. Nothing is new in this world, and occasionally, everyone does strange things. Ordinarily though, people will tend to remain constant in their behavior. Psychologically, a person will resist behavior changes, particularly if his past behavior has been satisfactory to him. In the case of your suspect, he will tend to repeat his behavior and resist any unusual act. If you are alert, as the suspect talks you can spot these points for further exploration. Further, it is well to keep in mind what you would like done and what you would dislike being done if you were the suspect. Never pull anything on a suspect that you would find offensive or objectionable if it were done to you. There are a number of books about human behavior on the market, and it will pay you to read them and put the information into use in your interrogation development.

17. *Do know the law.* As you can imagine, whole books could be written on this subject alone. The law pertaining to confessions, statements, prisoner's rights, and civil rights alone could fill this whole book, plus many more. For the purpose of this book, however, I will give you some common-sense ideas you can start with to keep you out of trouble in the interrogation room. A more intense research, on your part, should be part of your continuing interrogation study program. The first recommendation I make is to always conduct yourself in a prudent manner. Your dealings with any prisoner should be conducted as though you were in a fish bowl, and this is especially true when you are interrogating. Usually, when interrogating a suspect, you have only this one chance to talk to him; but, what you say and what you do has to stand up to close scrutiny for many months. Make it right the first time and save

yourself and your department a lot of headaches. Be prudent in everything you do relating to your suspect, and you will seldom go wrong.

Since the hoped-for result of our interrogation is a confession, let us first establish what a confession is. *A confession is a direct acknowledgment of guilt on the part of the accused.* This confession can either be spoken or set down in writing, obtained any place within reason, obtained while the subject is either under arrest or not, obtained spontaneously or by questioning, can be tape-recorded, typewritten, handwritten, or not written at all. It can be obtained by anyone, at any time after the crime.

The one big "but" in all of the above latitude is that this confession must be freely and voluntarily given, without duress, coercion, promises of reward or immunity. And this is the part of the suspect's rights that you must strive the hardest to protect. Since your words cause the suspect to confess, you must be sure that you have not violated any of the suspect's rights. A confession is worthless if it is not fairly and properly taken. Some important legal facts that you must keep in mind as you talk to your suspect are as follow:

1. An accused should be offered counsel before the interrogation starts.

2. Never offer the accused any hope, benefit, or reward for confessing.

3. Time is of the essence. The sooner an admission is obtained, the better. Things such as sleep, eating properly, and use of available facilities become an important factor the longer a suspect is held. Too great a lapse between the subject's arrest and his arraignment can invalidate any results you may obtain.

4. Use of mental or physical coercion will always invalidate any results you may obtain.

5. Any promises of leniency or threats aimed toward obtaining a confession negates its use as evidence.

6. Continual interrogation vitiates a confession.

7. A confession unlawfully obtained renders one made later, while the subject is still being held on the same charge, inadmissible.

8. Remember that the burden is on the state to prove, by a preponderance of evidence, that the confession is voluntary. Anything

that you do that would distract from this voluntariness will be detrimental to any later case.

9. Always read to your suspect a full and complete set of his rights as specified by the *Miranda* decision, before interrogation. The burden of proof of having advised these rights is on the "State." It therefore behooves you to be sure of this point. Read these rights from a printed form so you don't miss any, and then have the person initial the card with the time and date. This warning card, with the appropriate initials, should then be treated as any other piece of evidence, as it helps validate any confession you might get.

Warnings of Constitutional Rights

The Constitution requires that I inform you that:
1. You have the right to remain silent.
2. Anything you say will be used in court as evidence against you.
3. You are entitled to talk to an attorney now and have him present now or any time during questioning.
4. If you cannot afford an attorney, one will be appointed for you without cost.
5. Do you desire to consult with an attorney first or to have one during this interview?
6. If, at any time hereafter, you wish to remain silent or have an attorney present, all questioning will be stopped.
7. Has anyone, at any time, threatened, coerced, or promised you anything in order to induce you to make a statement now?
8. Do you understand these rights?
9. Do you wish to talk to us at this time?

The above list is not a complete synopsis of the regulatory laws affecting the interrogator, but if you will follow this list, you cannot go too far afield. By further exploration into the laws that affect the interrogator and the confession, you can refine your knowledge as to the limits of the law that you must stay within. It does you no good to obtain a confession improperly; therefore, thoroughly learn and follow the regulatory laws concerning criminal confession and rights of your prisoner.

You will probably find many more positive do's that should be incorporated in this list. This is as it should be, since this book is designed to introduce you to interrogation, and lead you to the point where you can confidently take over on your own and add to your own skill and ability. The list of do's are designed to lay the basic groundwork for your beginning efforts, and to start you down the road to a successful career as an interrogator. By further and deeper interrogation study, you can develop from this basic foundation to a competent and skillful interrogation level, but it takes study and work on your part. At this point, I will discuss the recommended don'ts individually.

DON'T

The don'ts are detailed in the following list.

1. Don't discourage the suspect. Nothing has a more harmful effect on your suspect, and on your contact with him, than discouraging him. If he becomes too discouraged, it will produce the "it will do no good to tell him" attitude. Your interrogation is designed to produce a positive act of admitting what he did. A negative attitude on the part of the subject tends to drive him further into his own remorse, and further from the point where you can talk to him. A person involved with too much introspection ("turning inward") does not have much perception left over to be aware of what you are saying. By encouraging the suspect to talk rather than discouraging him, you will get your confession. A discouraged person has no will to cooperate, and does not very often acquiesce to your urgings for a confession. This is not to imply that you should not discourage lying, since this is what you are trying to do in your interrogation. You should, however, not discourage the whole person to the point that you drive him within himself and out of your verbal reach. This requires tact on your part, but if you will put yourself in the place of the suspect and anticipate your reactions, you will ordinarily avoid any problems along these lines.

2. Don't antagonize or patronize. If your conduct with the suspect is such that you make him hostile toward you, it doesn't take any intelligence to see that you will not get much cooperation from him. One technique requires one interrogator to bait the suspect and leave the room. Since this is a basic interrogation book intended to instruct the beginning interrogator on how to conduct himself in the interrogation room, I strongly urge you not to pick

on or bait the suspect to the degree that you antagonize him. If you assume an antagonistic attitude toward the suspect, you can bet that he will return in kind, and this will in no way aid your getting him to cooperate with you. Avoid saying or doing anything that will upset or antagonize your suspect.

As to patronization, if we know that one meaning is "to be condescending," it immediately becomes apparent why we should avoid this kind of conduct. Nothing insults a person more than someone who takes a superior attitude toward him, and then appears to be giving the suspect a break by just talking to him. A businesslike, serious approach will not be insulting, but a superior air will be too much for most people to swallow. Again, the purpose of an interrogator is to convince the suspect he should confess, and he can only do this if the suspect believes that the interrogator is truthful and is actually involved in an interested, businesslike way. By patronizing a suspect, we only indicate to him that we think we are better than he is. This is certainly no way to gain his trust and confidence.

3. Don't pencil-listen. Nothing can scare a person away from a confession faster than an interrogator who comes in and immediately begins to take copious notes. If the suspect sees that everything he says is being taken down, he will begin to say less and less as you proceed. Taking all the notes right away only serves to remind the suspect of the seriousness of the trouble, and all of us have heard that "anything you say will be used against you in court." This is true, and it does no good to remind the suspect of this by your note taking. When you first begin to talk to him, keep the pencil and paper out of sight until you and the suspect have established a contact with each other. It is never a good idea to take a lot of notes in the interrogation room. If you must take notes, keep them very short, and only take them toward the end of the discussion. Following the interrogation is the time for enlarging the notes, not while you are talking to the suspect. Note taking only serves to remind him that you are an official trying to get him to admit something, and that you will use whatever he might say when you get into court. Don't pencil-listen if you can avoid it.

4. Don't ever act surprised at an admission. This point is some-

thing you will have to be alert to. I have heard suspects admit nearly everything a person could get involved in. Every so often, someone comes up with something new, and I must be careful to show nothing by my actions, other than an interested understanding. An interrogator must be particularly alert to this point when he is involved in sex crimes. I know we all find certain crimes and acts offensive, but if you are urging a suspect to tell you and you show disgust after he does, you can rest assured he will not tell you anything else. Most people who confess this kind of crime realize they have violated society's decency codes, and they will be embarrassed when they tell you. You cannot afford to scare them away from a complete confession because of your own prejudices toward the act. Your job is to get a total and complete admission; only by registering understanding and occasionally sympathy toward the suspect can you accomplish this. Never take anything said or done in the interrogation room personally, and you can then usually remain calm and composed during some disgusting admission. The truth is what you are seeking, and if you are successful in obtaining the truth from a suspect, you have accomplished what you set out to do.

5. Don't condemn. If you are to become a successful interrogator, you must not convey the idea to the suspect that you are the judge of what he did. All criminals, unless they are insane, are aware of what they have done, and are further aware that it was against the law. Most give every excuse as to why they committed the offense, and resent most people who take a condemning attitude toward them. As interrogators, we want them to believe we are interested in them and are trying to get them to do the best thing for themselves. Condemning the suspect for his act alienates him, and usually ruins any chance we have of getting him to cooperate with us.

6. Don't appear to dominate. This point will take some acting on your part, as you must dominate the interrogation if you intend to get results. The use of subtle control will be far more effective than a brash, authoritarian attitude, and you will appear in a far better light in the eyes of the subject. A person under arrest is already aware of being controlled, and we need not add to this feeling of oppression. Most of us resent being too controlled, and will fight back if it becomes too rigid. Mr. Clinton Duffey, former warden of

San Quentin, said in his book, *88 Men and 2 Women,* that he never knew of a single person who liked being in prison. As interrogators, we must control the interrogation but in a manner which does not appear to dominate. A quiet, dignified manner removes some of the sting of being directed, and a business-like, professional attitude indicates to the suspect you are, in truth, interested in him as a person, not as just another prisoner. Your conduct should be like an "iron fist in a velvet glove."

7. Don't be impressed by the subject's social or economic position. All of us are subject to being awed by someone in a high place or someone who possesses extreme wealth. As an interrogator, we must not let this feeling influence how we conduct ourselves. We are search-ing for the truth, and regardless of the person's position or wealth, he might be guilty of a crime. If we enter the interrogation room determined to find the truth, the person we talk to becomes the object of our conversation, rather than someone we look up to or down on. Occasionally, the suspect himself reminds you who he is and this, in itself, is a good indicator of his uneasiness. Rich or poor, high or low, we all get into our pants one leg at a time. Interrogation is our profession and we know it better than he does and, therefore, there is no need to feel inferior to anyone. I have found that a good equalizer in an interrogation room, when talking to someone of affluence or influence, is to call him by his first name only. Most people in higher stations of life are used to having tradespeople, and people who work for them or depend on them, call them Mr.————. We don't want to put ourselves in the position of appearing to be beneath them on any score, and so the first name. In reverse, if you want your suspect to perk up a little and act a little more digni-fied, call him Mr.————. This makes the suspect feel you respect him, and builds his ego up to the point where he may confess.

8. Don't ever make any promises. You may hear several interpre-tations of this suggestion. One is never offer a suspect any promise of reward or immunity for a confession; don't promise to help if he cooperates, but any other promise is OK. I have also heard it said, never promise anything you can't deliver. My sincere suggestion is never promise anything at all. There cannot be any halfway about this item, because anything you promise to do for a suspect can be

interpreted by the suspect as an inducement for him to cooperate. I know of two convicted felons who won retrial on this point alone. They interpreted what was said to them as a suggested promise of assistance, and that is why they confessed. Never promise anything, and you cannot get into trouble along these lines. If you do anything for the suspect, leave it unspoken; he will know that you have helped, but you will never have to defend any of your actions if you never make any promises of any kind.

9. Don't ever threaten. Under no circumstance should you threaten a prisoner in any way. You shouldn't do anything that is even suggestive of a threat. As we said earlier, the appearance of guns, cuffs, clubs, and so forth, in the interrogation room, can be interpreted as a threat; so can many gestures, intimations, and actions on the part of an interrogator be interpreted as a threat. A quick way to lose an entire case is to let a defense attorney bring out the fact that his client was threatened by the police. We are trying to win them with words, not violence. The use of threats indicates a lack of ability on the part of the interrogator; never threaten a suspect in any way.

10. Don't ever use coercion. The word "coerce" means to compel or force. Compelling or forcing a suspect to confess completely violates his constitutional right of not having to testify against himself. So, if we employ any kind of coercion with the suspect, it absolutely destroys the free and voluntary aspect of any confession he might give. A lengthy discussion on the point is not necessary, as it is completely apparent that you can never force a confession and expect it to be legal. If you are tempted to force any kind of confession from a suspect, remember that you not only violate his individual rights, but you lay yourself wide open to prosecution for violation of the Federal Civil Rights Law.

11. Don't be guilty of duress. Duress is generally thought of as a "state of mind" or "emotional strain" or "emotion distress" sufficiently compelling to force the suspect to confess. Fear on the part of the suspect is an example of duress. Anything the interrogator says or does which affects or influences the mind of the suspect to the degree that he is beyond his own choice of complying or denying, can be construed to be duress. Duress is primarily a mental state of force,

whereas coercion is primarily a physical state of force. Both vitiate a confession by causing the courts to consider them unreliable.

12. Don't ever strike or manhandle a suspect. Again, I feel that it should be unnecessary to mention this "don't." However, I suspect that even in these enlightened times there are still interrogators who resort to these tactics. If you are a beginning interrogator, you had best forget that this practice ever existed, and if you see or suspect that you will ever become a part of this kind of brutality, leave the room right away. Nothing, in my opinion, exhibits a man's inadequacy or ignorance more than conduct of this kind. I don't feel we need to discuss the legality of this type of behavior, because it has always been illegal and should always remain so. Never, under any circumstances, resort to any kind of physical violence directed toward your suspect, as you will be dead wrong with absolutely no excuse for this kind of conduct.

13. Don't deny him the human comforts he is entitled to. What I am suggesting here is that your suspect is entitled to use the bathroom occasionally, eat at regular times, drink water occasionally, and have all of the other human necessities that we all are entitled to. Because the suspect is under arrest does not mean he is less of a man, regardless of the crime under investigation. The law indicates that a person is innocent until proven guilty in a court of law. It is as much a requirement on the part of the police to protect the guilty as it is to protect the innocent. Certain human comforts are the protected rights of a citizen, and we should never derpive our suspect of any of them. I am not suggesting that you coddle the prisoner or bend to his every whim, but I am saying that you are obligated to afford any suspect certain human comforts that we all are entitled to. Probably the least important part of this fact is that it will look better in the eyes of the court. If we intend to retain any self-respect, then we must extend the human comforts to any suspect we contact. No man is an animal, and he must never be deprived of our understanding and solicitude as long as he remains reasonable.

14. Don't deny him his rights as provided by law. At the present time, the federal examination of the civil rights of our citizens is undergoing some agonizing scrutiny. At the time of this writing,

the struggle is still in process and, therefore, I cannot say what the outcome will be. However, certain civil rights are in effect now, unchanged by time, and will not be affected by the pending legislation. We have already discussed some of them—freedom from duress, coercion, violence, and oppression, human dignities, and others. Among other guarantees are the right of a suspect to counsel before he is questioned and makes any admissions or statements, the right of not testifying against himself, the right of speedy trial, the right of no invasion of his privacy, the right of knowing the reason for his arrest, and many, many other rights. All of these rights are designed to protect the dignity of our citizens. Violation of these rights on the part of any person in authority reduces us from a democracy to a police state. You and I, as interrogators, with our direct contact with a suspect can play an important part in the protection of his rights, which in turn protects our own, and has a small part in the preservation of our democratic way of life. I would suggest that you obtain from the library, or from an attorney, a complete accounting of the civil rights of our citizens before you start into this interrogation business. Again, I feel that if you will conduct yourself as a prudent man, you will be able to avoid any problems should some question you do not know the answer to come up. On your part, prudence in your conduct will ordinarily prevent a lot of trouble by never allowing a troublesome situation to develop, and if it does, by causing you to arrive at an intelligent solution.

To summarize this section in a few words is to say "avoid impetuous actions, words, ideas, and conduct." There is nothing new in either of these lists, but I have brought together some important "do's and don'ts" for you to examine.

Most of the foregoing list can be applied to any contact between two people. This is an important fact in itself, in that you are contacting another human being in your interrogation and all the rules of social conduct will apply, regardless of the persons's crime. The lists contain proven suggestions, and I am confident that if you incorporate these suggestions in your technique, you will benefit from it. Your interrogation technique begins with your first contact with the case, not just your conversation with the suspect. Your entire preparation, first contact, interrogation, and departure is part of the total picture of your technique, and you should constantly try and improve all parts of your ability. It will make very little difference how smooth you are with words if you have alienated the suspect, or done something that will invalidate a confession. No one has built-in finesse during his first interrogation. It all has to be learned and developed. By arming yourself with these few basic facts ahead of time, you have eliminated some of the fear of the unknown. Smoothness comes with practice, by application of the above facts, and by application of the various techniques that you will learn in further study.

Chapter 5

INTERROGATION FACILITIES

Now we come to a discussion of where to interrogate. This will often depend on the situation, but let's discuss one thing at a time. My recommendation is always take the person you intend to interrogate into surroundings not familiar to him. The very best place, naturally, would be a special interrogation room at the station house. However, sometimes this is impossible, thus the suggestion of unfamiliar surroundings.

To get a person to confess, you will have to plant the idea in his mind that it is the best or only thing for him to do. Where he is will have an important bearing on this implantation. If he is in familiar surroundings, he can draw some comfort from them, and resist your interrogation better. If there are people around listening, he will be too embarrassed to talk. If he is on the job, he will constantly be reminded of the full implication of his confessing. To alleviate many of these outside preventive influences, you, the interrogator, must pick the spot where you will talk to the suspect. The spot must be quiet so he can hear you and you can hear him, and should be where no outside noises will distract from the conversation. The spot must be private so he will not be embarrassed by others hearing you. There must be no outside distractions. Privacy also suggests intimacy, and this is helpful when talking to certain suspects. Finally, the spot must be apropos. I mean by this that a confession in the doorway of a sweat box will surely be considered to have been given under duress.

Since most interrogations will take place at the police station, let us examine what an adequate interrogation facility should be.

An interrogation room should be a place set aside for interrogation purposes only. Nothing else should be stored there, no equipment should be in the room. In other words, this room should not be a storage facility. Not only will piled up junk be distracting, but it will also lead to interruptions in the interrogation as people go in and out. The room should be of adequate size so as not to appear too small and oppressive, but not too large either. Smallness gives a person a closed-in or cell-like feeling, and this distraction alone can keep him from concentrating on what you say. On the other hand, too large a room allows the person a feeling of freedom. We all know the different sensations we have when standing in a large hall as opposed to standing in a closet. The room we want should be of an ordinary room size so as to suggest nothing, neither closeness nor expanse. Again, there should be nothing outstanding about the room so as to catch the attention of the suspect; no extremely high ceilings, or mismatched walls, or uneven floors, or other construction peculiarities. If you have a window in the room, try to avoid having bars or mesh wire exposed to the sight of the suspect. This suggests imprisonment and slows down the interrogation procedure. Either cover the window with a drape or blinds, or, at the very least, place him so he does not look at the barred window.

The walls should be painted a pastel, relaxing color that will tend to calm rather than excite a suspect. Imagine what a cool, restful, green room would be as opposed to a room with bright red walls, and you will see what I mean. Certain bright colors have a definite psychologically stimulative value, where others act as a depressant for excitement. You will notice that hospital uniforms and walls have been recently changing from white to a pale green. This was done as a result of a color study that determined that patients seemed to be more relaxed in the soft pastel-colored room than in a stark white room. In our interrogation room, we also want to achieve this relaxed attitude as far as subject tension is concerned, and so the suggestion of the pastel colors. Further, it is a good idea to avoid too many colors in the room. The whole attitude of a room is established by the color, and if you have a rainbow-type room, it tends to be distracting rather than relaxing.

It is my suggestion that the interrogation room should have rugs on the floor. This may seem like an extravagance, but I believe that it is worth the expense. A rug should be of some neutral color, plain design, and adequate to cover the room. Avoid a flowery, loud rug for the same reasons you avoid loud paint. A bright, flowery rug can also be distracting if it doesn't fit the decor of the room. You are striving toward a relaxing, calm room, not one that excites. The rug need not be expensive, but neither should it be a shabby, excessively used one either. Rugs suggest a business-type atmosphere, and further remove a suspect from the police atmosphere. Rugs also tend to muffle any outside noises and absorb some of the sounds inside a room. It is far easier to confess in a calm, quiet room than in a noisy, confusing room.

The matter of soundproofing is pretty much up to the individual. It is my suggestion on this matter that if you do soundproof, only put enough material on the walls to absorb most of the noise. A room should never be absolutely soundproof because this in itself is oppressive. The soundproofing should be such that it muffles outside noises rather than eliminates them completely. A few muffled sounds of outside life is a good idea, as it eliminates from the mind of the suspect the fear of being absolutely alone.

It makes no difference how nice the inside of your interrogation room is if it is not kept clean. If the room is allowed to grow shabby and dirty, this in itself indicates to the suspect that the work of the department is that way also. Shiny cleanliness indicates an alert, interested approach to people. Dirt indicates just the opposite. There should be no excuse for dirty, smudged walls, dirty, spotted rugs, or floors and accumulated "junk" lying around the interrogation room. It takes very little effort to keep the room clean if it is used exclusively for interrogation, and the results obtained by using a clean room will justify any expenditure of energy to keep it that way.

You may hear many suggestions about furniture in an interrogation room. Probably all of them have merit, but since this is my book, I will include only my suggestions. I have mentioned previously that you should eliminate any table or desk between you and the subject. Of course, it would be ridiculous to have a room with just two chairs in it. I suggest that a table be put in the room, but in such a position as to prevent it from coming between you and the suspect. A table can serve as a desk for statement signing, can hold evidence and serve other purposes as conveniently as a desk. I am opposed to a desk in an interrogation room because of the fact that a desk usually represents officialdom, and serves as a reminder of the fact that you are in a police station. Also, we all would be inclined to sit behind the desk, and this again would only serve to remind the suspect of the official nature of the investigation. The chairs in the room should be comfortable and neat, without being too soft and effeminate. Use regular office chairs without arms, rather than some over-stuffed chair, kitchen chair, bedroom chair, or the like. Try to have all of the furniture match if you can. A tip that could be helpful is to try to have the subject sit in a chair a little lower than yours. This has a psychological advantage in that he will have to look up to you, and will afford you some little advantage in keeping control of the situation. Above all, keep the furniture neat, appropriate, and at a minimum.

Avoid all ornaments and wall pictures in the interrogation room. They are distracting to the interrogation, and lend nothing to the interrogation technique. Often, a suspect can concentrate on some object, or an object may remind him of something completely foreign to the matter at hand. Leaving the ornaments or pictures out of the interrogation room deprives the suspect of any superficial comfort he might obtain from their presence, and further insures that he will have to concentrate on your words alone. An observation mirror is a different matter and should be considered a necessity. Place it as inconspicuously as possible, and see that the subject does not look directly into it. Try to place it so that the viewers will be in a room different from any hall or room that serves as an entrance to the interrogation room. This viewing room should also contain any recording equipment. It never does any good to remind the suspect that the mirror is a two-way type; however, if he inquires, tell him the truth without hesitation. I often tell a man that when we talk to women, we have to use it; or, when talking to a woman, I say that in the case of dangerous felons, we have an observer there to prevent any escape. Most people are aware of this type mirror, and if you attempt to become cagey, they will suspect that you are lying to them. You lessen your interrogation potential when this happens.

Your room should be adequately lighted. If it is too dim, it is suggestive of skulduggery, and if it is too bright, it suggests third degree. The best bet is some indirect lighting fixture, the same as in any other office. A naked light bulb should be completely eliminated. Frosted fixtures or fluorescent lighting is the best idea.

If you have an interrogation room, make sure it is adequately cooled in the summer and heated in the winter. Anything you can do to insure that the subject does not suffer any physical discomforts will insure that you will have that much more of his concentration on your conversation. In an uncomfortable room, neither the suspect nor the interrogator can fully concentrate on the matter at hand, and neither will be at his best or be able to last as long as in a comfortable room.

Let me include a small drawing of what I think a good interrogation room should look like. I will not use the recommended color scheme, but you can see from the drawing (see Fig. 3) what I have in mind. Remember, this is only a recommendation, for I know each reader will have his own particular physical plant to contend with. But, by the inclusion of as many of these ideas as you can in your room, you should be able to come up with a fairly adequate interrogation room.

Occasionally, you will be forced into a situation where you will have to talk to a suspect in the field. I feel that it is a poor idea to ever interrogate in the field. There are always too much distraction and noise that can ruin any chances in a further interrogation. Usually, you will have the opportunity to ask your subject to come to the office and talk, and if you do, always wait until you are in the interrogation room before you really push your interrogation.

Probably the only place outside the interrogation room that it is good to push your interrogation is at the scene of a crime that has just been committed. While the subject is still filled with the heat of the moment, his defense will often be completely down, and he will not have had time to think of either the ramifications of what he has done or to make up any excuses for the act. It pays at that time to ask him, "Do you know who did this, John?" Often, without even thinking, he will come out with the full story which will be extremely hard to refute at a later date. If he does come right out with the story, pursue it to the end and get all of the facts. An oral confession is as good as a written confession; if you get the confession orally, you ordinarily can follow up later with a written one.

FIGURE 3

INTERROGATION ROOM

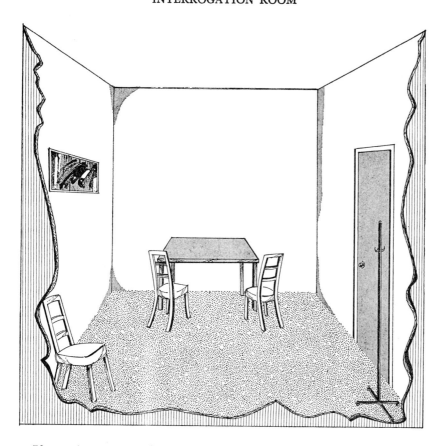

If you have successfully gotten the suspect in a car, then with a little more effort, you can usually get him to accompany you to the station. I never think it is a good idea to seriously interrogate a suspect in a car, especially in a police car. Everything about a police car is suggestive of authority, from the radio blaring every few seconds to the flashlights and nightsticks lying on the seat. Trying to talk to a suspect in your automobile just makes it more difficult for yourself. If you must talk to your suspect in the automobile, park the car, face the subject, turn the radio off, and put all of the police paraphernalia away, or at least out of sight. At best, interrogation in an automobile is poor, so do everything you can to improve it.

Interrogation in a place of business can be equally as frustrating, as the person you are talking to will usually be familiar with the surroundings. This is a fact you must overcome if you expect any success in your interrogation. If the person you are talking to works in the shop or is a laboring man, make arrangements to talk to him in some office that he ordinarily does not frequent. If he is an office worker, try to talk to him in the president's office or some other place where he does not work every day. If he is the president or manager of the firm, invite him to your office. In order to be successful in your interrogation, you must remove the suspect from familiar surroundings and away from friendly faces. We all draw some strength and comfort from these things, and you want your suspect to be paying full attention to you, not looking for friends or listening for friendly, familiar sounds or sights.

Lastly, if you intend to interrogate on the street, take the suspect to some quiet out-of-the-way place where you will not be constantly disturbed, to a doorway, alley, or something similar. Place him so that he must look at you, and so that he cannot look beyond you or over your shoulder and see movement or people. Again, the street is a poor place to interrogate, and you should avoid it if you can.

The main item to keep in mind is that you need privacy to properly conduct any interrogation. It will make no difference how much you know about the case, about the suspect, or about interrogation principles if you do not choose the right place to talk to the suspect. I would say that no single item we have discussed, in and of itself, would be enough to make a person confess. But put them all together, and you reinforce immeasurably your chances of successfully concluding your interrogation. Making sure that everything is right in the interrogation facility is part of your interrogation technique, and will afford you successful conclusions more often than not. All of the little things that you do are what will win for you. You must be attentive to every angle of this interrogation business if you intend to succeed.

Chapter 6

HOW TO BEGIN

THE GREETING

W<small>E SHOULD</small> now be ready to walk into the interrogation room. We have gotten all of the facts of the case; we have researched the background of the suspect, and we have in mind all of the interrogation principles that are available. It is now time to open the door, enter the room, and start the interrogation.

I have cast about in search of an idea as how best to present this chapter on "How to Begin." All kinds of suggestions have been made, but I believe the best one would be to actually make this a case report. Accordingly, I will present a hypothetical case report and background research, and then include the interrogation just as it would proceed in an actual case. You must remember that this will be a hypothetical situation; names, dates, places, and facts will all be fictitious.

As we go along in the case, I will interrupt the scene now and then to include a discussion of what we have accomplished, and also to insert some alternate ideas of how to approach the same situation. I feel that a more complete explanation can be made if we inspect a real case as we proceed along with our interrogation. By following the case and by using the facts in the case, we can actually see how things go in an interrogation room. Once you have seen the ideas in action, it should be easier for you to put them to your own use in real-life practice. So now let us study the case file as it is laid on our desk for us to work on the interrogation. (See Figs. 4 through 9).

We now have the case in hand, and are ready to prepare ourselves for the interrogation. Let's just review what we found out by reading this case report. Remember that these facts will have to be committed to memory so that when we enter the interrogation room, we will not have to keep referring to the case report itself. Let's look at the request form first. (See Fig. 4.)

FIGURE 4

REQUEST FOR INTERROGATION

TO: Interrogator, Police Dept.   Date: 5-20-71

Name of Person and Office making request:_____Tame_____

Subject's Name:_____Karl Clayton_____

Race__W__Sex__M__DOB__11-6-47_____   FBI RECORD: Yes__No_X_____

Has interrogation been discussed with the subject; if so, explain:

_____No. Suspect arrested 9:30 P.M. 5-19-71_____

Nature of Investigation:__B&E_____

Felony_____X_____Misdemeanor_____Defendant or Witness__Def.

Name of officer in charge of case_____Tame and Smith_____

Brief statement of facts regarding case:_____

_____Sam's Place was hit during the night of 5-18-71. No visible___

_____means of entry. Thief probably was locked inside. Cigarettes___

_____and phonograph records stolen. No damage done as record_____

_____machine and cigarette machine left open._____

_____

_____

_____

_____

                                        R. E. Tame_____
                                        Requested By

                                        Sgt., Criminal Investigation
                                        Title & Dept. Bureau

FIGURE 5

OFFENSE REPORT

COMPLAINT NO._____ | Complainant SAM'S PLACE _____ Serial No._____

Address 1 W. Church St. City _____ Phone: home GA 1-2345 Office 246-8100

Offense B&E BUSINESS _____ Reported by Sam Little, manager _____

Address 810 E. Terry _____ Phone: home same Office same

Place of occurrence 1 W. Church St., City _____

Reported to Sgt. Chandler , at 12 N. m, 5-19-71 , 19____, by Sam Little

Date and time (at or between) 2:30A.m., _____, 19____, and 2:30 A.m., 5-19-71 , 19____

Officers on scene Sgts. Tame and Smith _____

Persons attacked _____

Property Attacked Cigarette machine and juke box, also 10 records (see list on reverse side)

How attacked Removed cigarettes from opened machine

Means of attack Hands, cardboard box

Object of attack To obtain cigarettes and records

Trademark _____

Vehicle used _____

Persons arrested SUSPECT: Karl Clayton
2203 E. Main St.
City

Details of offense (state fully all other details of offense and investigation): Complainant advised that they had been broken into so much they leave their cigarette machine and the juke box open at night, after taking the money out of it. This way, the machines are not torn up and it does not cost them any money to have them repaired and they do not suffer any loss. However, on this particular break, subject removed approximately 20 cartons of cigarettes, more or less. Main items were 4 carton Winstons, 4 cartons Pall Mall, 4 cartons Salem, 2 cartons Camels, 2 cartons Vic roy and 2 cartons Kents. These cigarettes are valued at $2.85 per carton. Als removed were 10 records from the juke box. The names of records removed are listed on the reverse side of this report. It is believed this subject was locked up in the building and after everyone left, he helped himself to the cigarettes, placing them in a box and then left the building. It is unconfirme however, information from a B. Ogelthorpe is that someone called him and advise that they saw a Karl Clayton leaving the building sometime after they closed at 2:30 A.M. this morning. At the time he was leaving, he was seen carrying a cardboard carton. It is our understanding that someone spoke to the man and he made the statement that he "was cleaning up inside." We have attempted to contact B. Ogelthorpe to substantiate this information with negative results. More work to follow on this case.

Unfounded ____ eso ☐ Signed Sgts. Tame and Smith ____ Date May 19, 1971
Cleared by arrest ____ ☐ Investigating Officer.
Exceptionally cleared ____ ☐ Signed _____ Date _____

FIGURE 6

STOLEN PROPERTY REPORT

QUANTITY	PROPERTY STOLEN	ESTIMATED VALUE	RECOVERED DATE	RECOVERED VALUE
10	Records			
	#13-#14: Monkey Time, Mama Didn't Know (by Major Lance)			
	#11-#12: Oh, Baby Doll, Deep Down Inside (by Bob & Earl)			
	#9-#10: Pain in my Heart, Something Swaying Me (Otis Redding)			
	#7-#8: Nightfall, I'm Free (Al Hibbler)			
	#5-#6: I Need You So, Has My Love Grown Cold (Ted Taylor)			
	#3-#4: Talk That Talk, Ony You, Only me (Jackie Wilson)			
	#1-#2: Love me or Leave me, Something's Got to Give (Sammy Davis)			
	#19-#20: If I Look a Little Blue, Question (Lloyd Price)			
	#17-#18: Let Them Say, It Must Be Love (Ivory Joe Hunter)			
	#16-#15: What Made Maggie Run, Little Bit O-Boy (Del Vikings)			
		TOTAL		

DESCRIPTIONS OF SUSPECTS OR PERSONS WANTED

Name	Karl Clayton 21	
Alias		
Address	2203 E. Main	
Color, sex, age	White M 21	
Height, weight		
Eyes, hair	Bld Hr.	
Complexion	Ruddy to Light	
Nativity	American	
Occupation	Unknown	
Dress		
Other marks	Lives with parents	
Why wanted	Suspect in above offense	

FIGURE 7

ARREST REPORT

			OPD ARREST REPORT		
NAME CLAYTON	Karl	nmn			
LAST	FIRST	MIDDLE	ARREST NO.		
ALIASES					
ADDRESS 2203 E. Main					
OCCUPATION Waiter	Father		AGE 23	SEX m	RACE W
TYPE	EMPLOYED BY				
D.O.B. 11-6-47 P.O.B. Charleston, S.C.		PRIOR LOCAL ARR.? neg			
BOOKING CLK.	DKT NO.	ARR. OFF Smith-Scoyoc			
VEHICLE USED	MOTOR NUMBER	LICENSE NUMBER			

			RIGHT INDEX
CHARGES B&E			
	TELEPHONE USED YES NO		
LOCATION 2203 E. Main	TIME 9:30P DATE 3-19-71		
DISPOSITION			
WARRANT, YES NO	POLICE REPORT YES NO CIRCLE ONE		

FOLLOWING TO BE FILLED OUT IF SUBJECT'S PRINTS AND PHOTO ARE TAKEN ORIGINAL TO
BOOKING OFFICER 2ND COPY TO I.D.   3RD COPY TO DET BUR IF ASSIST REQUESTED

RECORD NO.	PRINTS PHOTO? YES NO	F.P.C.	
PHOTO NO.	REF. DET. BUR? YES NO		
PRINTS BY	WHO? TIME		
HT: 66" WT: 164 EYES: br HAIR: br COMPLEXION: med			
HUSBAND (OR WIFE) Single			
SCARS DEFORMITIES RIGHT OR LEFT HANDED TATOOS OTHER SOCIAL SECURTIY NO.			

FATHER:	C. Howard Clayton	2203 E. Main
MOTHER:	Mildred	"
BROTHER:	neg	
BROTHER:	neg	
SISTER:	neg	
SISTER:		
DETAILS OF ARREST:		

B&E Sam's

TO BE FILLED IN BY DET BUREAU

ASSIGNED: _____ CHARGES _____

DISPOSITION: _____ DATE _____ TIME _____

THIS FORM MUST BE TYPED OR PRINTED BY OFFICER

FORM NO. 602-02-1

FIGURE 8

GENERAL REPORT

General or Supplementary Offense Report	Date__5-20-71____ Time__2:15 P.M.__
	Old Case ☒ Juvenile ·☐ Other ☐
	Offense_____Serial No.___

Victim_____SAM'S PLACE_____Address___1 W. Church St., City_____

Additional details of offense and progress of investigation:

Supplement to offense report 5-19-71 by Sgts. Tame and Smith

RE: B&E BUSINESS, ABOVE, VICTIM

ARRESTED SUSPECT: Karl Clayton WM 23
                         2203 E. Main St.
                         City

May 19, 1971. At the end of our tour of duty, we requested
Sgts. Van Smith and R. L. Scoyoc to arrest Karl Clayton at
2203 E. Main whenever they possibly could catch him at home.
We had been by there earlier with no success in locating this
subject and we were advised that he should be there around
6:00 P.M.

Subject was arrested by Sgts. Smith and Scoyoc at 9:30 P.M.,
on the 19th of May.

This Form Used For Juvenile Offenses And Other Non-Criminal Reports

☐ Unfounded
☐ Cleared by arrest   Signed___Sgts. Tame and Smith___ Date__5-20-71_____
☐ Exceptionally cleared   Investigating Officer
☐ Inactive   Signed_____Date_____
                                           Commanding Officer

602 - 2 - 07- 05

FIGURE 9

PRISONER DESCRIPTION FORM

Record No._____

Date of Record_____

POLICE DEPARTMENT

IDENTIFICATION BUREAU
Prisoner's Description

New ☒   Repeater ☐

FPC_____

Name	First	Middle	Last	Address
	KARL	nmn	CLAYTON	2203 E. Main, City

Alias

COLOR	SEX	AGE	HEIGHT	WEIGHT	HAIR	EYES	COMPLEXION
W	m	23-71	66	164	bld	br	med

BUILD	FORMER ADDRESS	BIRTH DATE	BIRTHPLACE
med	145 E. Summerlane, City	11-6-47	Chasn, S.C.

OCCUPATION	EMPLOYED BY
Waiter	Father

MARITAL STATUS	DESCENT	"Come On Inn" 456 W. Circle
single	US	

	Name	Address	City	State
HUSBAND OR WIFE	na			
FATHER OR INLAWS	C. Howard Clayton	2203 E. Main		
MOTHER	Mildred Clayton	same		
BROTHER	n/a			
BROTHER	n/a			
SISTER	n/a			
SISTER	n/a			
FRIEND	Dicky Searcey, Cactus Rd			
FRIEND	Carlos Stackhouse, Bottle Drive			

Scars, Marks, Deformities	Tattoos
Scar Rght knee, cut left elbow	n/a

Education GS ☐ HS ☒ Coll. ☐ City Hi 65	Speech southern
Religion Prot. ☒ Cath. ☐ Others ☐	Remarks Lived in City since 6 weeks old
Prev. Arrests Yes ☐ No ☒	no Juv trble
U. S. Serv. n/a	

U. S. Serv. No. n/a	IN	OUT	

Type of Discharge	
Smokes L&M	
Drinks beer	RECORD TAKEN BY Celeste

A quick review shows that we are dealing with a young, white male, age twenty-three. He apparently has no FBI record, and we will be the first persons to interrogate him. We are seeking information on a felony: breaking and entering, and this suspect could possibly be the person who actually did the job. The offense was that someone stole cigarettes and phonograph records. Apparently, the thief did not break in and further, the thief did not do any damage to the place in the commission of the crime.

Digesting these facts in our minds, we discover some ideas we might pursue. Sam's Place serves alcohol, so the suspect could have had too much to drink, passed out, and been left there after they closed up. There does not seem to be an FBI record, so it might be that this is a first offender. Another support for the overdrinking idea is the lack of evidence of any sign of entry. Next, there was no damage done inside the place. This could suggest that the thief has frequented the place before and intends to return to the place again. Most people will not tear up a place that they intend to revisit. Further, if he has enjoyed his visits to the place, he will subconsciously avoid any damage that might close or destroy a place that he finds enjoyable. The theft could have been deliberate, but there is also a possibility that it was a spur-of-the-moment thing with opportunity making the above the thief.

Now let's review the case report itself and get the facts as the investigating officers found them at the scene of the offense.

First, we see that it was Sam's Place that was hit. We know that this is a club and is open to anyone. So this makes it difficult to single out any group as suspects, as anyone can enter. Further, we find that the thief struck sometime between closing time, 2:30 A.M., and re-opening time, 9:30 A.M. This is a lapse of seven hours, but these seven hours are at a time when there will usually not be large crowds on the street. It might be that someone saw the suspect moving around on the street in the vicinity of Sam's Place. Next, we see that a quantity of cigarettes and records were taken, coupled with the fact that the thief took them in a cardboard box. Again, because of the hour, it might have been that someone saw our suspect leave the place carrying a box. Not unusual, but it would certainly be conspicuous. Further, the theft of the records themselves would tend to indicate that the thief was young and still involved with records and dancing. An older person would probably have taken liquor or beer, but our thief took only cigarettes and records. Next, we see that it was a mixed lot of cigarettes, but that there were twenty cartons taken. This many cigarettes would have required a rather large container to carry them in, not something that could be slipped under the shirt or in a jacket. Again, a person carrying a bundle this big could have been seen. In referring to the list of records, we notice that the type music is such that it would appeal to a younger person's taste rather than someone older. We know that our suspect is young; so far, the facts that we have developed would tend to indicate that someone young had pulled this job. Sure enough, someone is reported to have seen our suspect leaving the scene with a box. This witness is further supposed to have talked to our suspect. By checking with the investigating officers, we find out that B. Oglethorpe is the bouncer at the club and he was supposed to have received the call. The witness is, as of yet, unconfirmed, but what he is supposed to have said is certainly supported by our analysis of the facts that we have developed in our own minds. A good thing to keep in mind is the reported conversation between the witness and the suspected thief. It might be important in proving to the suspect that we have him cold, and that he should confess to us.

Upon checking the follow-up report in the case, we see that our suspect was arrested on the same day that the offense was reported. This could mean that the loot is still intact. The suspect could have hidden it, but he probably would not have had time to dispose of all of it. Further, we also can assume that our suspect has not had too much to drink, as he was arrested early in the evening; and, unless he had been drinking all day, he will probably be in good shape for our interrogation. The arrest slip indicates that this suspect works in a restaurant, so he could have knowledge of cigarette machines and phonograph record machines.

A short synopsis of what we have learned so far would now be in order. Let's list it.

WHO:	Karl Clayton, WM, 23.
WHAT:	Breaking and entering.
WHY:	Theft of cigarettes and phonograph records.

WHEN:	Between 2:30 A.M. and 9:30 A.M., May 19, 1971.
WHERE:	Sam's Place, 1 W. Church, City.
HOW:	Apparently inside job. Suspect probably locked inside.
HOW MUCH:	About 20 carton cigarettes and 10 phonograph records.
WITNESS:	One reported witness who talked to above.

Now let us proceed further with preparing ourselves, and check our record system to see if they have anything on the suspect. A check of *central records* indicates no contact; a check of *traffic records* indicates no records; a check of *criminal records* indicates no FBI record, but we can look over the pedigree sheet developed by the identification officer.

In looking over this information, we can discover a number of things about our suspect. Right away we see that he is brand-new to our department. We can assume that he is a first offender, and we can deal with him accordingly. Further, we notice that he lives at 2203 E. Main, and that this is also the address of his mother and father. Since he is twenty-three years old and still lives at home, coupled with the fact that he also works for his father, we can assume that he is probably not an adventurous-type person; more than likely, he is mild mannered or even meek. The subject is also slightly over-weight, 164 pounds and 5'6", so all of this combined (living at home, working for father, probably being a somewhat retiring personality) could account for the lack of damage at the scene. A person will more often than not play out his personality at the scene of a crime. Since this suspect is new to the department, it also supports the contention that this could have been an "opportunity" theft rather than a deliberate, planned theft. We should check the records on the mother, father, and two friends listed on the pedigree sheet. The I.D. officer indicates *no record*. Again, this supports the opportunity theory in that this suspect does not associate with people that have been in trouble with the police. His high school education indicates that he has had enough self-pride to finish that much education, but either through lack of opportunity or self-drive had not had enough push to go further, or for that fact, even leave home. His high school education does indicate, however, that we will probably not have any trouble communicating with him. Finally, we notice that he smokes, which could support the theft of cigarettes, and also, that he drinks. This could be the reason he was in Sam's Place. All in all, we have something of a picture of our suspect now, plus a picture of the crime, and more importantly, we have in our minds a picture of why this person is a suspect in this crime.

Now it is time to go in the interrogation room and talk to him about this offense. We have plenty to talk about in that we have some knowledge of his past behavior, past history, employment, education, and many other items that we can discuss, plus we have the facts of this crime.

This part of the book concerns the "Hello," so in this chapter we will get the conversation going with our suspect. I will try and explain just what we do each step of the way and you will be able to see how it was done in this case. With a little imagination, you can apply the same techniques, or similar ones, to the cases that you will deal with. In order to add a little realism to this part of the book, I will include the conversation in question and answer form just as it would have occurred in the interrogation room itself. The only interruptions will be an occasional explanation of alternate methods, or other ideas that should be included.

Let's set the scene. Our interrogation room has all of the previously described attributes that a good interrogation room should have. Our suspect has been in jail all night and slept, according to the jailer. He was served breakfast, and appears to be in good health. He has been brought to the interrogation room, and is in there now waiting for us to enter. It is about 8:30 A.M., and we know that the suspect has not been abused and has been afforded all of the humanities he was entitled to. So we assume a serious attitude, enter the interrogation room, and meet the suspect for the first time.

Interrogator: "Good morning, Karl, how are you this morning?"
  (Shake hands.)

Suspect: "OK."

Interrogator: "Karl, my name is Marshall Star, and I have been asked to work with you this morning. First, let me show you my credentials, and tell you that I work here in the bureau. Karl, according to the Constitution, I am required to inform you that

1. You have the right to remain silent.
2. Anything you say will be used in court as evidence against you.
3. You are entitled to talk to an attorney now, and have him present now or at any time during questioning.
4. If you cannot afford an attorney, one will be appointed for you without cost.
5. Do you desire to consult with an attorney first or to have one during this interview?
6. If, at any time hereafter, you wish to remain silent or have an attorney present, all questioning will be stopped.
7. Has anyone, at any time, threatened, coerced, or promised you anything in order to induce you to make a statement now?
8. Do you understand these rights?
9. Do you wish to talk at this time?"

(Show the suspect your credentials.)

"Did you get something to eat this morning?"

Remember to keep it serious and businesslike. I feel that it is best to let the suspect know who you are so he knows just exactly who he is dealing with. He already knows he is in jail, so it will not come as too great a surprise that you are a detective. It is best to soft sell what you intend to do. So the inclusion of the words "work with you" shows that you need his help, and that jointly, you can accomplish something of purpose. I purposely left out the word "detective" from my place of employment. The use of words of authority have their own damaging effect, so I used the word "bureau," and let him draw his own conclusions. I might have used "department" or "this office" and achieved the same effect. The question about breakfast was used to steer the conversation temporarily away from the object of the interrogation. It allows me time to size up the suspect; and, also, it allows the suspect to become familiar with me and my voice and actions.

Suspect: "Yes, they fed me."

Interrogator: "It sure isn't like Mother's cooking, is it?

What did they have, eggs or something else?"

The reference to "Mother" is quite deliberate. The beginning of the interrogation is the time to size up your subject. If you can use certain words to check out certain ideas right away, so much the better. We suspected that this person attached a lot of significance to home and parents, so what better way to see how this question affects him? Always try your ideas out, but be subtle and believable. Further, always try and ask questions that require more than Yes and No answers. The faster we get this suspect talking, the sooner we will get the confession.

Suspect: "We had eggs, and they weren't good."

Interrogator: "Karl, I understand that you work for your father as a waiter. Is this your only job?"

Suspect: "It's the only job. I only work for him part-time, just when he needs me for parties and stuff."

Interrogator: "How do you get along with your dad? Some guys can't seem to work for their parents."

Suspect: "We get along OK. I have been trying to get some other job, but just can't seem to get one, you know."

We have now gotten the suspect to come out of himself a little. Most people will be hesitant to talk right at first, and the interrogator must inject some subject in the beginning that the suspect can talk about. You must make this seem like part of your total picture of interrogation. It must be natural and not appear to be a deliberate effort to cause the suspect to talk.

If your suspect in this case were someone who had been in prison or a lot of trouble before, you would not pursue this exact line of questioning. The introduction would be generally the same, but you would avoid, to begin with, any really personal questions. You could inquire into things such as how the job was going, how the family was.

Other openings to the conversation might be the following:

Interrogator: "Good morning, my name is Star, and I was told that you are Karl Clayton."

or

Interrogator: "Hello, I'm Marshall Star. Your name is?"

or

Interrogator: "Hi, you're Karl Clayton, aren't you?"

Remember that the opening must be serious and believable. You have to get off on the right foot, and you want to start warming up the suspect right away. For the first few minutes, after the opening, you want the conversation to be general and easy with the suspect. He is judging you, and you, him. So give both of you a few minutes to relax. Always include the civil rights warnings in the very beginning.

Back to our case. We are in the first few critical minutes of conversation during which you must avoid any harsh discussion or argument. Try and use what you have found out about the suspect in order to keep the conversation going freely.

Interrogator: "How far did you go in school, Karl?"

Suspect: "I graduated here in the city. High school."

Interrogator: "What kind of work are you trying to get into, Karl?"

Suspect: "I guess I will stay in restaurant work. My dad says that I can get on full time as soon as business picks up."

Interrogator: "It must be kind of tough to live and have any money, just working part-time."

Suspect: "I make about 20 to 30 dollars a week most of the time. I live at home, so that doesn't cost me anything."

We have again gotten the suspect to come out of himself somewhat. If you will notice, we have gotten him to talk more than the interrogator. This is what we want him to do. By allowing him to talk more than the interrogator, we know that he will be volunteering information, not just answering questions. In order to get any confession, the suspect must be talking and volunteering information. The subject matter in the beginning is not important, as long as it can flow naturally and easily, and allow the suspect to respond. Another point to remember: Don't ever forget that everything, even during the light conversation in the beginning, must have some bearing on the case. In other words, no wasted conversation. In the above dialogue, we have checked for reactions to his mother and dad, attitude toward work, and his financial position. It all has been light and easy; but, by being alert, we can check for any sensitive areas as far as suspect reaction.

Interrogator: "Karl, I noticed on the report that you were picked up about 9:30 last night."

Again, I think that the words "picked up" have a less harsh sound than "arrested" or "booked." Avoid as many threatening words as you can during all parts of the interrogation.

Suspect: "Yeah, two detectives came to the house, and brought me here. They said that I was being arrested on probable cause of a felony, whatever that means."

Interrogator: "That's what I want to work out with you this morning, Karl. I believe that you and I, together, can get this trouble straightened out. We are both mature adults, and can successfully get this business worked out. I know that your parents are both successful and hard-working people, and I believe that you will do everything in your power not to let them down. Trouble is not new to anyone, you or me or anyone else, so why don't you tell me what you know about this situation?"

It is my opinion that when you are talking to a suspect, you should not refer, in the beginning, to the crime itself. I believe that it is best to call it the "business" or "situation" or "problem." If the suspect then admits anything, you know that it is voluntary information on his part, as you have not suggested anything to him. Another personal opinion of mine is that the word "think" should not be used by the interrogator. "Think" can be interpreted by the suspect as guesswork, and you want him to believe that you are confident of your opinions. A final point is that you should always inject into the beginning of any interrogation the question, "Why are you here?" Quite often, the suspect will come right out and admit the whole thing; and, even if he doesn't, you haven't lost anything. I personally believe that a short buildup helps in presenting this question, and so the above reference to the parents of our suspect. I could have talked about truth, responsibility, reality, or anything else along these lines. In this case, we can recall that this is a young, first offender who has probably lived a sheltered life, and so the inclusion of parents.

Suspect: "I don't know what you are talking about. Those men who brought me from the house said very little, and I don't know about any break-in at all."

Interrogator: "Someone took some merchandise from a place uptown night before last, and we want to talk to you about it."

So now we have the interrogation opened and going. We have gone in, introduced ourselves, found out something about the suspect and his attitudes toward the entire situation, and have gotten him to talking with us. We have gotten through the first few minutes of the conversation with him, during which we caused him to talk casually with us—in other words, to open up a little and speak a few of his own ideas. The primary purpose of the opening is to get the suspect talking to us. By being casual in the beginning few minutes, we can steer the conversation around to the subject of the interrogation in a natural manner. Never appear abrupt or in a hurry. Make everything that you do seem natural and easy. In order to win the confidence of your suspect, you must appear to be natural.

There are other methods of opening interrogations, but I believe that in the beginning you should develop this natural approach. Wait until you have a little practice with people before you turn to anything more advanced. It is far easier to practice and become smooth at this natural approach than to learn the more difficult ones that involve a lot of acting on your part.

Make the beginning of your interrogation businesslike and confidential, just as you would expect to be treated by a professional man that you called on. The words that you use are not really important as long as they have some bearing on the case, and mean something to the end result of the conversation. You can cover your own feelings of nervousness by just simply starting the conversation about some subject that both of you have some knowledge of.

Some suspects that you talk to will require a much longer period of this warm-up than others. Don't ever rush the suspect. Take as long as is necessary to get the suspect to come out of himself. You want him responding and volunteering information before you proceed into the meat of the interrogation. It will do you no good to start right in on the interrogation if he is just responding with grunts. Whenever you get the suspect talking over longer periods of time than you do, it is a good sign that he is coming along. Then, and only then, is the time to bring up any reference to the "trouble."

The remark about "patience" made previously was not idle conversation. A good interrogator is a patient man who will take enough time to bring his suspect along at the proper speed.

Chapter 7

KEEP IT GOING

An extremely important factor in all interrogation is that you must keep the conversation flowing smoothly, and without jerky breaks or interruptions. I imagine that all of us have been involved in a conversation with someone and recognized that the conversation was forced on both parts. This is something that must never creep into an interrogation. The conversation must appear to be relaxed and easy, never forced or strained. In any conversation, if both sides are uncomfortable with the situation, the idea of termination is uppermost in both parties. Therefore, the interrogator must develop the habit of keeping the conversation moving from one subject to another in an apparently effortless manner.

There are methods and aids to help the interrogator to achieve this even flow of conversation. Basically, the problem to be avoided is to become self-conscious in the presence of the suspect. This is no small problem. Ordinarily, practice will overcome this feeling, but even a beginning interrogator can help himself by knowing a few tricks that will help eliminate this reaction. Probably first and foremost is that the interrogator must know the case completely. By knowing all of the facts about the case, you know exactly what you are after, and, therefore, need not worry about some unknown aspect of the case cropping up. Further, a complete background check of the subject will furnish you with a world of conversation material about your suspect. In our case we can talk about the local schools, his restaurant work, his parents, what kind of work he is going to do in the future, among other things. By keeping the conversation on a low-pressure level in the beginning, you can let the talk flow along as you become adjusted to him and the situation of interrogation. Never underestimate what the records or background check can give you. By being armed with some built-in conversation pieces, you can keep things going smoothly as you gradually ease the suspect toward the purpose of the interrogation. If he backs off, you can still be armed with things to talk about if you know this person's background thoroughly.

This segment of the book will be about how you can keep the conversation running smoothly. An easy-running conversation is what you want in order to get the end result, a confession. If there are abrupt halts and apparent searches for words on the part of the interrogator, it will be very obvious to the suspect that he is not very able in his art.

During this part of our interrogation, it is the proper time for the beginning of the various interrogation techniques. I will not go into these various methods of convincing the suspect to talk, as I feel there are a number of excellent books on this subject. I would suggest that you get any of a number of these interrogation technique books, and study the various approaches and ideas they suggest you use for convincing the subject to talk.*

By integrating these techniques with the basic approaches that we are learning, your ability to seek out the truth should be greatly enhanced. I am not implying that by simply going in and talking in an effortless manner you can get the confession in every case. I do say, however, that you need the smooth approach, coupled with the basic knowledge of interrogation, plus the more exotic techniques to get the confession in the majority of the cases. It takes a combination of all of these things to be a good interrogator and your entire techniques suffers if you omit any part. Therefore, I will discuss a few proven ideas that will in no way interfere with your techniques for keeping the suspect talking and for keeping the conversation headed toward your desired goal. Again, the idea that I am trying to get across is to keep it smooth and easy and apparently effortless. You, the interrogator, must control the attitude of the interrogation, and it is in your hands to keep the tone easy—easy for you to proceed and easy for the suspect to confess.

---

* This list in no way includes all the books published on this subject, but it will serve as a starting point for your further studies in interrogation. Inbau and Reid: *Criminal Interrogation and Confessions,* 2nd ed. Baltimore, Williams & Wilkins, 1967. Inbau and Reid: *Criminal Interrogation and Confessions Study Guide.* Santa Cruz, Davis Publishing Company, 1968. Weston and Wells: *Criminal Investigation—Basic Precepts.* Englewood Cliffs, N.J., Prentice-Hall, 1970.

HOLD OFF IDENTIFYING THE DETAILS OF THE CRIME AS LONG AS POSSIBLE

To me, this is extremely important in your relationship with your suspect. By avoiding the introduction of the specific details after the full *Miranda* warning, you can serve a number of useful purposes. As already discussed, if the suspect does mention any details, this, in itself, suggests to the interrogator the suspicion that his suspect is the party that he is after. Further, it serves as a test of the suspect's cooperation. If the suspect is sincerely trying to straighten everything out with you, his volunteering of information will indicate that he is truly desirous of cooperating. Occasionally, you can uncover other crimes that the subject confesses to if identifying the specific details about which you are trying to learn is avoided. It has always amazed me that people will confess to other things to help clear themselves of a more recent crime, but it does happen. My partner and I interrogated a suspect one time who confessed to seven breakings and enterings over the past six months, trying to convince us that the "problem" we were investigating last week was not his fault.

Another important feature of avoiding discussion of the crime facts is that it keeps the mention of official matters at a minimum until long after the conversation between you and the suspect has become easy. You, the interrogator, should have already established your contact with the suspect and should have established "rapport." A harmonious or sympathetic relationship should have already been established. Every time the official nature of the interrogation is mentioned, it only serves to remind the suspect of the reason for his arrest, and should, therefore, be held off as long as possible. By keeping the conversation on a general level, you do not hurt your chances for the confession, and you do help yourself by allowing yourself and the suspect time to understand each other better.

LET THE SUBJECT TALK

If you have not proceeded too fast, by the time you get to this part of the interrogation your subject should be talking freely and volunteering information. As you discuss the problem of his arrest, he will begin to talk more and more, if you allow him to. Again, the problem of the interrogator comes into play. Most people would rather talk than listen, and this is something you must overcome if you are to become a good interrogator. If you have presented your case correctly to the suspect, he will usually be more than willing to talk. Do not interfere with his talking, other than to keep it along the general lines of the direction you are going. The more he talks, the more apt he is to make a slip or even to talk himself into admitting the offense. Usually, the subject will become very animated in his conversation once you have told him the reason you are talking to him. He will want to explain everything that he did if he is giving you an alibi; if it is a downright lie, most people will talk and talk just to make sure that you believe them. A few guiding questions on your part will usually serve to keep the suspect talking. Of course, if he begins to stray away from the subject at hand, then you must interject just enough corrective conversation to redirect the conversation.

It is my opinion that the subject should be allowed to talk as long as he wants to discuss the incident at hand. Some subjects, in order to avoid the crime, will talk about everything under the sun except the incident itself. As you listen to the suspect, be attentive to his every word, so that you can break into the conversation if he gets lost. It is better to stop him before he thinks that his evasive conversation is effective, or before he gets his mind altogether on another subject. However, as a general rule, if you get the suspect talking and telling his side of the issue, you will be far better off than if you do all the talking. If the suspect is talking, you will have time to think about the case in total and decide what you are going to do next. It takes practice to talk and think about something in advance at the same time. A suggestion is that when you have to interrupt to get the subject back on the track or want to introduce a new question to him, make every effort to make the break or question sound sincere and as if it were part of the conversation. Do not abruptly change the subject or start off on a new track. It makes the conversation rough and might make the suspect suspicious of what you are attempting to do. Further, it also makes it appear as if all of the suspect's foregoing conversation was meaningless. If you are to win the confidence of your suspect, you must avoid making him suspicious of your words and manner.

GET TIME ELEMENT INVOLVED

One of the best ways, and also a way to make it easier for the suspect to talk, is to have him go, step by step, over the activities of the time in question. By sequencing his actions, it allows his thoughts to achieve some order and, at the same time, allows you to check the story as you know it should be. If your suspect is jumping from one time of day to another, back and forth, the story loses any continuity, and both you and he become confused. If you will direct the conversation so that one thing follows another in its proper order, you can gradually build the story up to the point where you have a complete understanding of the situation as the events occurred This act of sequencing the events will occasionally have another beneficial result. As the suspect proceeds along with his story, step by step, he is, in effect, building himself up towards a peak at which he will either deliberately lie about committing the crime or admit to the crime. Occasionally, the suspect will talk himself into the admission as he goes along with his story in this item-for-item manner. After he has gone through his original explanation of his side of things, you should also discuss one thing at a time, and let everything stay in order. You will never accomplish anything if you both become lost in a maze of facts. By a few adroit questions, you can usually get your suspect to thinking along the lines of the step-by-step type of story.

LET THE SUSPECT MAKE HIS ORIGINAL EXPLANATION WITHOUT OBJECTING

After you have told the suspect what you want to talk about, he will usually have a full story to tell you concerning what his actions were on the night or day in question. It is the best idea to allow the suspect to give his first explanation without interrupting or objecting to what he has to say. By allowing him full rein, you can see the direction of defense that he intends to take, and you can also pick out the points for discussion that you care to. By knowing the case fully in advance, you will be able to know when he is lying or, at least, recognize the points that he has omitted that would be important to the case. By letting him go through the case first, you can review the whole situation with him, and you will know about what is coming next. Further, if he then begins to change his story to fit the facts of the case, you will know that he is lying, and you can then push for the confession. Do not take notes during his original review of the case, for he will be less anxious to talk if he sees you writing down what he has to say. Be alert and hear everything that he says, and make your notes later. Listen for impossible situations to develop as he talks, or for long lapses of time in his activities. Both of these usually indicate that it is a point about which he is trying to conceal information, or possibly, completely cover up. Further, by listening to his complete story before beginning to suggest that he has not been completely truthful, you allow that much more time to elapse before you have to test the rapport you have established with the suspect. If you have done your job well, the rapport will stand the strain of his knowing that you do not believe him, and he will continue to talk. If you have not done your job properly, he will probably tell you "where to go" and stop talking altogether. So, allow as much time as you can to build an understanding between the two of you.

START TALKING ABOUT THE TIME PRIOR TO THE CASE

The very best way to really cover a crime is to start the conversation about events that occurred prior to the commission of the crime itself. This serves to set the scene for the buildup to the point of confession. Occasionally, the suspect will give much usable information during this period of his discussion. Quite often, usable evidence can be discovered if the suspect is allowed to discuss, in full, his actions leading up to the commission of the crime itself. A total discussion of the suspect's activities will serve to inform you of every event in this subject's activities, and also proves to the suspect that you are thorough and conscientious in your research. If you notice that the suspect is leaving large gaps in his recount of his activities, stop the story and ask him to explain what he did. Occasionally, your suspect will be responsible for a series of crimes, and you will want to find out about all of them. Break your conversation down to the day of the crime, then to the hour; as you come closer to the actual crime itself, obtain a minute-by-minute accounting of his activities. Be alert for the physical possibilities involved in this time research. Try to imagine how long it would require you to do the things that he says he did, and see if his story is reasonable and believable. By being alert to this point, you can quite often obtain many more facts from the suspect than if you had overlooked the comparison. Pursue the activities of the suspect from prior to the crime all the way through the crime itself and, if appropriate, right up to the time of his arrest. By following through, you can occasionally find out this person's contacts and M.O., and this, in itself, could be productive to the case at hand, or any future cases you might have. Remember that no time is wasted in the interrogation room, and everything should have a purpose. By being complete in your interrogation, you build a sound and adequate accounting of the suspect, his time, and his activities for yours and the investigator's analysis. Be sure to thoroughly research every part of your suspect's activities and have him account for everything that he did. It is not good enough for him to say "I stopped and got gas and then went on." Find out where he stopped, if he saw anyone that he knew, and so forth. All of this might be just what you need to put him in the area, or might involve the time element. Be alert and get all of the facts in each case that you interrogate.

ASK ABOUT ANY OTHER CRIMES

Never shut the door, during any part of your interrogation, to the suspect's admission of any other crimes he might have committed. If he does admit anything, take account of it, but pursue your immediate goal. Often, a person will admit to something of a lesser nature to get you off the track of what you are after. If they do admit something, fine, so much the better, but keep after what you went in for. Don't be thrown off by an admission of something other than that which you are looking for. Often, an admission of this type indicates that the suspect is withholding what you want and is testing to see if he can throw you off.

Now that we have a few ideas and suggestions for keeping the conversation rolling along, let's try them out in our case. We should be able to keep this interrogation going along by applying some of the suggestions that we have just read.

As you recall, we have started the suspect talking and have sug-

gested to him that something was taken from a place uptown. Let's
see how it would work out in this case.

Suspect: "Well, I sure didn't take anything."

Interrogator: "I am not saying that you are the one who took anything. All I am doing is checking things out to see just what
happened. Maybe what we better do is for you to tell me just
what you did the night before last."

Suspect: "You want to know everything I did?"

Interrogator: "Yes, suppose you start with the daytime, and tell me
what you did. If I have any questions, I'll ask them as we go
along."

Suspect: "OK."

(The suspect then generally accounts for his time up to the time
he was arrested. He states that he worked until 6 P.M., ate, and
then went to Sam's Place around 8:30 P.M. He had two or three
beers, and then went to his girl's house about 11:30 P.M. She
wasn't home from a party she had gone to, so he laid down in
a hammock in the yard and went to sleep. He awoke about 7 A.M.,
went back uptown, ate breakfast, and went home. He went to
bed, slept till about noon, and stayed around the house until the
officers picked him up and brought him in.)

The general review of the case by the suspect was put in here in
this manner because, as you recall, during the original review by
the suspect you do not interrupt or argue the facts with him. Full
rein on his conversation allows him to become that much more
accustomed to talking, and it also allows you time to analyze his
defense. By a quick review at the end of his story, we can see that
his story is weak; however, we will also be hard put to prove that
he did it if he doesn't confess.

Now is the time to start back over his complete story, step by step,
and have him fill in all of the details that he omitted the first time
through.

Interrogator: "Karl, you said that you worked that day. Who do
you work for?"

Suspect: "Dad. I worked in the restaurant up till suppertime, then
I ate and went to Sam's Place."

Interrogator: "What time did you eat, Karl?"

Suspect: "About six, I guess."

Interrogator: "Where did you eat supper?"

Suspect: "After I got off work about 5:30 or 5:45, I went with Dickey Searcy over to Tom Cooper's place, and I ate there."

Interrogator: "What's Tom Cooper's place?"

Suspect: "The Sailor's Bar on San Diego Street. We had a couple of beers and I had a sandwich."

Interrogator: "How long were you in the Sailor's Bar, Karl?"

Suspect: "Not too long. Searcy had to go home 'cause he had a date with his girl, Penny, so he left a little after six."

Interrogator: "What time did you leave the bar?"

Suspect: "A little bit after he did, ten minutes maybe. I didn't have much money, and I was going uptown in the evening, and I wanted to save some."

Interrogator: "When you left the bar, where did you go?"

Suspect: "I went home. Ma was there, and got mad as hell 'cause I had missed supper, and she could smell the beer."

Interrogator: "What time did you get home?"

Suspect: "About 6:30, I guess."

As you will notice, I have broken the times down to the point that I know, at least up to this point, where he was every minute of the time. This kind of review serves two purposes. One, it helps me understand step by step what he did, and secondly, it allows him to volunteer more and more information. Once you have the suspect talking, try to keep him going as long as it is in the right direction. The more he talks, usually, the more relaxed he becomes, and he drops his defenses more and more. If you will notice, in his conversation up to this point we have developed two important facts that we can use later. Remember, we wondered in the case review if this wasn't possibly an opportunity theft. We now know that our suspect was drinking from about 6 P.M. on, and that he might have gotten drunk and committed this crime. Further, we know that he did not have much money with him. This might prove an important factor, as it could be a motive for the theft. Let's take him a little further along and see what we can find out.

Interrogator: "How long were you home?"

Suspect: "About an hour, I guess. Ma was raisin' hell, so I took a

bath, changed clothes, and took off. I was going to eat and bor-
row some money from her, but I didn't 'cause she was mad. I
just cleaned up and came uptown."

Interrogator: "How did you get uptown?"

Suspect: "I got the 7:45 bus at Hillside and came up to the Church
Street stop."

Interrogator: "What time was this, that you got uptown, I mean?"

Suspect: "I think it gets in at ten minutes after the hour. When I
get it home, it leaves at fifteen after the hour, and it is always
sitting there ready to go."

We now know that the suspect is fully in the swing of things by
his volunteering the information about the bus schedules. He is cooperating so far, so let's continue.

Interrogator: "What did you do then?"

Suspect: "I went to Sam's and had a beer. I stayed in there until I
went over to my girl's house."

Interrogator: "Did you see anyone in Sam's that you knew?"

Suspect: "Sure, lots of guys. I fooled around in Sam's, playing the
pinball machine, and drank a few more beers until about 11:30
when I went over to Kelly's house."

Interrogator: "Who did you see that you knew, Karl?"

Suspect: "Oh, I seen Carlos and a lot of other guys. Some of them
I don't know the names of, I just know them when I see them.
You know. I know lots of guys that I don't know the names of,
plenty of people that you meet you don't. . ."

Interrogator: "How many beers did you have, Karl?"

Suspect: "I don't know. Maybe three or four. I didn't have much
money, maybe three or four dollars."

Interrogator: "Were you drunk?"

Suspect: "No. I was a little high, but I knew what I was doing all
the time. I know that I left there alone about 11:30 and went
to Kelly's house."

Interrogator: "Who is Kelly?"

Suspect: "My girl, Kelly Lynn. You ain't going to talk to her, are
you? She didn't even know I was at her house, and she don't
know anything that I did last night at all. She was over at Gail
Tisdale's house at a party, and didn't even know I was at her
house. I don't want her to know I'm even down here."

Again, this suspect has reinforced his story about leaving the place before it closed, and about going to sleep. He also is claiming that he was sober and knew everything that he had done on the night in question. This is important to remember, because if he changes his story, we can remind him of the fact. Also, we have opened up two very good interrogation wedges that we can use later. One is that we can offer him an excuse for his actions by having too much to drink; secondly, we can use his feelings for his girl friend as a wedge. This is getting into the field of interrogation technique, and I am offering them here to show that this is the part of the interrogation during which you can determine the technique you will use later on.

As you study books on technique, you will see many, many approaches that can be made with the information we are developing now. But all the techniques in the world are useless if you haven't brought your suspect along properly with basic interrogation practices. Unless you can bring your suspect up to the point where he is cooperating with you and is receptive to your interrogation suggestions, you are wasting your time. This part of the procedure, the initial research of his story, is the all-important research period to determine what line of questioning you will later pursue. Do not ignore or sell short this line of basic questioning. Usually, it is a matter of rather routine questioning, but if you are alert to his words and any changes or emphasis that he places on his words, you can almost see the proper line of questioning to pursue as it develops. When you do hit a stop in his story that looks like it might produce the desired results, store it for later use and continue on until you have a detailed accounting of his activities, and then pick up the points to interrogate. We have also found another person to check with to determine our subject's condition at the bar. These points are good to note, because if this suspect does not tell us anything, we may have to prove it if we can. Every person who was a witness to his actions may be a key factor in proving this suspect is, in fact, the guilty party.

To review a little at this point, you can see that we have yet to reveal the actual crime itself. It still is defined by us as being only "trouble" or "the problem." Even though we are involved deeply in the interrogation procedure, we have not revealed anything. Always protect the facts of any crime that you are working with to the best of your ability. Withhold as much information about it as you can from the suspect. It might be that he is guilty and will not admit it. Further, if he does admit to you that he did the crime, you can check the veracity of his confession by comparing his words and actions against what you know to be true. Recently, I got a confession from a man in reference to a case of hijacking. His accomplice admitted to the crime and, when faced with this admission, the other party finally said he also was involved. We knew that the first contact with the hijacked truck was in a little town not much more than a spot in the road. Both parties named the wide spot, and we knew that both were telling the complete truth since only the participants would have known the name of the place. Hold out as much as you can so you can check your confession for completeness and truthfulness.

We are allowing the suspect to continue step by step with his story and to recap all of his activities on the night in question. Notice that we started the conversation about the time prior to the actual offense. This step allows us to build up to the actual offense, and further shows us a complete picture of our suspect.

Now, let's return to our interrogation in progress. All along, we are building the time element toward the time that the offense actually happened. Further, we are testing the subject's story for weak points for later interrogation. We are checking for holes in his story and making him account for any witnesses that may turn up later in the investigation. As yet, we have not questioned his story and have not tried out any specific interrogation techniques designed to cause him to confess. We are still establishing, in detail, what his alibi is.

Interrogator: "I might have to ask your girl if she saw you in the swing. That's all, Karl. Nothing else that I know of right now. By the way, what time did you say you left Sam's Place?"

Suspect: "11:30. I left at 11:30 and went to Kelly's place, but she wasn't home, so I laid down in the swing and was going to wait for her to come home. I must have gone to sleep. I didn't see her at all, and the next thing I knew, it was morning with the sun shining."

Interrogator: "Did anyone see you leave Sam's, or did you leave with anyone?"

Suspect: "No. Carlos had already left, and I didn't see anybody I knew. I was by myself when I left."

Interrogator: "How far is it from Sam's Place to Kelly's house?"

Suspect: "I don't know."

Interrogator: "You have some idea, don't you? How about just estimating it for me?"

Suspect: "About eight or ten blocks, I guess. I never really checked it."

Interrogator: "Did you see anyone as you walked along that you knew, Karl?"

Suspect: "No, I didn't see anyone. It was 11:30, and most everybody was off the streets 'cause I didn't see anybody—just some cars passed me, is all."

Interrogator: "How long did it take you to walk there?"

Suspect: "About a half hour, I guess. I don't know for sure. Why? What happened? Was I supposed to have done something?"

Interrogator: "Let's get the rest of the story, Karl, and then we will go over what the report was, OK?" (Suspect agrees without words.) "What is the address of Kelly's house?"

Suspect: "127 North Kraft Avenue. You aren't going there, are you? Don't get her involved 'cause she doesn't know anything."

Interrogator: "Know anything about what, Karl? What do you mean 'she doesn't know anything,' Karl?"

Suspect: "I mean, she doesn't know I was at her house. She never saw me, and I left before anybody got up and saw me. That's all I mean."

Interrogator: "You say it took you thirty minutes to walk to her house. Did you stop anyplace on the way there?"

Suspect: "No, I went straight there and laid down and went to sleep. It was pretty late and I was tired. I had worked all day, and then I didn't get no supper and had too much to drink. I went right to sleep, and I didn't see anybody, and nobody saw me, I guess."

Interrogator: "OK. What happened next?"

Suspect: "Well, I woke up and the sun was shining in my face. I got up and walked back uptown. It was about seven when I got back uptown. I was walking by Sam's Place and I seen the door open, so I went inside the door 'cause I wanted to get something to eat. I didn't see or hear anybody in there, so I left and went on to Jackie and Len's to eat breakfast."

Interrogator: "You say you went in Sam's Place and didn't see anyone?"

Suspect: "Yeah. I seen the door open, and they usually don't open until about nine or ten. I looked in and didn't see anybody, so I figured they were cleaning up or something, so I left and went to the restaurant and got some coffee."

Interrogator: "Did you look in Sam's Place, or did you go clear inside the place?"

Suspect: "I took a few steps inside the door, but I didn't see anybody, so I figured that they weren't open, so I left right away."

Interrogator: "Did you touch anything or take anything from Sam's when you left there?"

Suspect: "No. All I did was look inside the door. Well, I stepped in the door a little bit, and then I left. I sure didn't take anything from there, and I didn't touch anything either."

Interrogator: "How come you went in there at all?"

Suspect: "I saw the door was open and I though somebody might be in there I knew or something. I know Sam Little, and I thought he might be there."

Interrogator: "Did you see anybody on the outside, or did anybody on the outside see you, Karl?"

Suspect: "I didn't see anybody at all. I saw a guy on the street, but I don't know his name."

Interrogator: "What time did you get to Jackie and Len's restaurant?"

Suspect: "About 7:30 or 7:45, I guess. I had some coffee and then got the 8:15 bus, and went home and went to bed. I was home when the police came and got me."

Now we have a detailed accounting from our suspect of all his activities during the time in question. Certainly, as we have gone along, we can see that there are some weak points or holes in his story. These items are the ones that we marked down mentally to go back and pick up later. The points we intend to pursue are how many beers he had (to give him an excuse for his actions), his statements of being broke or nearly so (to give him a reason for stealing), the time gap in his arriving uptown in the morning and eating break-fast (as being an opportune time to steal), the first statement of his about sleeping in a hammock and later a swing, being inside Sam's Place in the morning (as being the time), and last, the original report of a witness. All of these items are worthy of our attention, and should come in for some detailed interrogation. We need answers for all of these points, and the answers must be related to time, be appropriate, and fit into the text of his alibi. By going back over each item and getting a full, detailed accounting of his activities, we can fill out his story to the best of our ability.

We have promised to explain to our suspect what we actually suspect him of at the completion of his story. I feel that the best time to go into this point is after the explanation of activities, if it is possible to hold off that long. You will run into situations in which you will have to explain the charges right away to your suspect in order to keep him talking. I don't feel that you should ever argue with your man over this point, as it is his right to know what he is charged with. However, keep your explanation to a minimum, and hold as many of the particulars as you can in confidence. This is not a point important enough to create a conflict over, but I feel you will benefit by being sparing in your offerings of information. Don't be pumped.

If you have brought your suspect along and have his accounting of his activities, time enough has passed to go over the specific charges with him. After you have had him explain all of his movements and explain away all of the holes, then you can go over the charges with him. You might introduce the crime itself in the following manner:

Interrogator: "Karl, someone took cigarettes and records from Sam's Place after they closed up last night. With you being out all night, we feel you know something about it."

or

Interrogator: "Karl, Sam's Place was broken into last night. Since you were seen there early this morning, you can see as well as I that someone might think it was you."

or

Interrogator: "Karl, we have a report of a theft from Sam's Place during the night. Since you were there last night and also early this morning, there is a possibility you might have made a little mistake and gotten drunk and taken the stuff. How about it?"

You can see that the introduction of the crime was designed to let the suspect talk, if he was so inclined. Never, or at least try and avoid asking any Yes or No questions. Give your suspect some opportunity to talk and to make his denial or admissions in more than one word. You may have to reveal the crime at any time during the interrogation, but when you do, design the words so they will provoke more than one-word answers.

After obtaining the alibi from the suspect and introducing the crime, it is time to go into the techniques you will learn, and discuss evidence and witness testimony that you might have. You will, by the time you reach this point, have your suspect's story down pat, have him talking freely, have yourself at ease and under control, and have the whole interrogation flowing along nice and smooth and easy. Occasionally, you will talk to a suspect who will be a quiet, reserved, or rather hesitant type. If you feel that he is cooperating to the best of his ability, then he, too, should be led along, with you doing most of the talking. The test for progress in interrogation is suspect cooperation. If you have his cooperation and you have established that nebulous "rapport" with him, you are on your way to success. If you try to go along too fast for your suspect, when you come to the critical part of "did you or didn't you do it," you will not have your suspect prepared properly. Don't rush, take your time; make sure that you have the time to take before you even begin your interrogation procedure. Time and patience are the all-important factors, plus skill and practice. This combination is what makes the good interrogators good. You can't rush headlong into the interrogation situation and expect to accomplish anything in just a few minutes. Sometimes, it doesn't take much time to get a confession, but this is the exception rather than the ordinary situation. As our case has progressed, we are now deep in our interrogation techniques. We are employing all of the various methods we know to convince the suspect that he should tell us about the crime. We are making all of the proper suggestions, and employing all of the psychological levers that we have available. All of these various techniques are available to you for further study from other sources. Our purpose here is to show just how to get you to the point at which you can apply these more refined methods in your quest for the truth.

Avail yourself of all the facts of the case, then try to keep the conversation at a general level. If you have to mention that a tool was used on the window, refer to it as a "tool." Never say it was a screwdriver, or a tire iron, or whatever else it might have been. By saying a "tool," the subject can corroborate your words and indicate his truthfulness in a confession by saying what it was he used. Keep any suggestions of a specific item out of the conversation if it has any bearing on the case in question. Also, protect your witnesses' identity to the best of your ability. Say "a person," but never say "John Doe." Keep any references to real things on a general level. Further, always protect the source of any information you might have. To the best of your ability, avoid any discussion which would even indicate or suggest the source of your information. The suspect does not need to know everything you know, and does not need to know how you got your information. In your refusal to answer any questions, make it reasonable or understandable why you won't answer. Don't just say "It's none of your damn business," but rather "You know I won't tell you. It wouldn't be fair." or "I'm sorry, but I just can't answer that one." The suspect knows he probably won't get an answer to his question anyway, and by answering decently you won't alienate him.

So, I have just about concluded this part of the book on "keeping it going." By applying these suggestions, you should be able to bring any suspect along to the point at which you will be able to cover his alibi and have him relating to you his excuses and activities. Each individual case will bring about different problems, but each will also have enough similarities that you can use these general suggestions for keeping the suspect talking. Occasionally, you will meet someone who will not fit the picture at all; however, most people you meet will fit the picture of Karl. By cooperating to the extent that you can, you can get him talking to you if you go carefully.

Let's look back into the interrogation room and see how it's going.

Interrogator: "Karl, we have a report that someone saw you leaving Sam's Place carriyng something. How do you account for that?"

Suspect: "I didn't carry anything from there. The only time I was in there was just long enough to look in, and when I didn't see anybody, I went out again."

Interrogator: "Did you talk to anybody as you left the place?"

Suspect: "No, I only saw one guy, and I don't remember saying anything to him. Find him and you'll see that I didn't take anything, 'cause he can tell you."

Interrogator: "Do you know who the person was that you saw?"

Suspect: "I've seen him around, but I don't know who he is."

Interrogator: "What time did you see this person?"

Suspect: "Just after I stepped back out of Sam's. About seven or a little bit after, I guess."

Interrogator: "What did this person you saw look like, and how could we talk to him?"

And so it goes, with the continuing questioning of your suspect. By having him explain everything he saw and did, you will get a complete picture of his activities. Also, as you talk, the pressure is building up in a guilty suspect and, at any time, he might just come right out and admit the thing. Be alert for any sudden changes or for any exaggerated activity on the part of your suspect as it will usually preceed the confession. Don't act surprised or overanxious at these times, but continue to question and get the full story from your suspect.

An interrogation goes along only as long as the interrogator can keep it going. It is up to you to keep the conversation flowing. By arming yourself with some ideas and methods for keeping the words coming, you will succeed where others fail when arriving at the point where they "can't think of anything else to say." In all of your conversation, you must keep two things in mind: keep the suspect involved and talking, and keep the conversation calm and moving smoothly. Think ahead and plan what you are going to say next, or consider what idea you will investigate next. Don't babble or talk in a rush. Avoid excitement and hysterical approaches as it only serves to excite the suspect. Can you imagine how the person felt as he was flying along high in the sky and then heard the pilot begin to laugh hysterically? When he asked, "What's the joke?" the pilot said, "I'm thinking of what they'll say at the asylum when they find out that I've escaped." Avoid this kind of excitement and keep everything smooth and low in pressure as long as you can. You can't afford to be a "Silent Sam" and interrogate. Consequently, you should always use good technique in your interrogation. This means keep the conversation flowing.

Chapter 8

CLOSING

THE TERMINATION of any interrogation should be with the hoped-for confession. All too often, however, this is not the case, and so we must consider how to close our interrogation properly. This chapter is not intended as a panacea for one's failure to successfully interrogate, but will provide a sampling of some ideas for your use after every other effort has failed. Never forget that some of the people you come in contact with will be telling the truth in their denial of guilt. Further, there are some guilty persons who will be able to resist all of your efforts and will make no admissions. These people fall within the category of persons who should receive the benefit of these closing suggestions. Every interrogator has some special method of closing that has proved successful for him in the past. By mentioning a few here, I can pass on to you some of the thoughts along this line, and you will be able to adapt all or part for your own use.

That every part of the interrogation must be considered as to its effect upon the subject and how it fits in with the total picture of your interrogation is a point important enough to reiterate. Nothing must be wasted in your interrogation—neither your words or your time. Therefore, consideration must be given to the technique of how to close your interrogation.

I believe the best piece of advice I ever received on this subject was that when you have exhausted every method that you know, tried everything that you can, and still haven't gotten the admission and are ready to give up—try just one more time. I have found that this has served me admirably over the years. In the first place, it will prevent you from giving up too easily as is the case in most interrogations. If things don't seem to begin to click right away, it's easy to say "Well, he won't go anyway, so I might as well quit." By using this "one more try, one more time" adage as a rule of thumb, you might find that the extra effort might be the one that gets the desired results.

After you have tried once more, then, and only then, should you consider how to terminate the conversation. A point to remember is that when you have decided that further conversation will be fruitless, never reveal this to your subject. If he is the guilty party and has resisted your efforts up to this point, the minute that you reveal that you are weakening and ready to quit, he knows that he has you beaten. We have already mentioned the fact that a lie once told is easier to repeat. The same holds true here. If your suspect has defeated you, he will find it easier to resist the next person. Consequently, the next interrogator will have to work just that much harder for his confession. Everything that you do will have a direct bearing on your suspect, and you must always protect yourself and your associates by being thorough and complete in your interrogation workmanship. If you intend to become a competent interrogator, you must include the words "thorough workmanship" in your planning and working effort. Leaving anything undone that should have been done in your interrogation means you have failed yourself and your profession. This is not to say that anyone will deliberately prostitute himself by deliberate effort or intentional omission. I am suggesting that through thoughtless or careless attention to the continuity of your interrogation, the closing or cessation of the immediate effort is too often overlooked or sloppily done. By prior consideration of this part of your interrogation effort, you can eliminate this fault in your interrogation technique and thereby enhance your interrogation ability.

The desired result of your interrogation efforts, naturally, is a confession, so always make the final effort along the lines of securing acknowledgment of guilt. If you have gotten to this point without an admission, it goes without saying that your suspect is denying everything. In your final attempt for your confession, you should gently overlook this fact and proceed on the premise that he is just on the verge of confessing and you are attempting to help him over this final hurdle. Often this is the case, and after this final drive for the confession, he will come out with it when you were not really aware of the fact that he was ready.

The word "gentle" should be kept in mind in this final effort, because it has more than one importance. I have seen interrogators come out of the interrogation room with their faces flushed and red, and holler back, "You better come across 'cause you're looking through the prison doors right now." For all practical purposes, both the subject and the interrogator are lost to each other, because both have lost any possibility of contact with each other. This business of hollering at each other at the end of an unsuccessful interrogation is nothing more than an admission on the part of the interrogator that he was inadequate and could not secure the confession. He gets angry and the subject gets angry, and the whole thing goes up in the air.

By gently disregarding the subject's protestations of innocence, you do not go so far as to agitate him or to leave him with a bitter feeling towards you. You suggest that you are not convinced that he is innocent and that you are sincerely desirous of his coming clean with you. Let me offer a few examples of this point to explain what I am driving at.

Interrogator: "Listen, Karl, we have talked for quite a while about this situation, now why don't you get this whole situation cleared up with me without any more fooling around?"

Interrogator: "You know, Karl, I still believe that there are some problems in this case that you need to straighten out and now is the time."

Interrogator: "Look, Karl, you and I both know that this business has got to be straightened out. Why don't you go ahead and admit it while you have the opportunity and let's go from there?"

What you have done is suggested to him that you do not believe him, yet you have not come right out and accused him of being a liar. You have given him a final opportunity to confess and have shown him that you are still sincerely interested in seeing him get himself "squared away."

The second reason for being gentle in your closing is that you should always leave yourself in a position of being able to talk to the subject again, either about the same thing or something else. If you walk out ranting and raving, hooping and hollering, you will never be in a position to convince him again that you are sincere and truly interested in him and his problem. He will always remember that the last thing you did was leave in a cloud of fire and brimstone, accusations, hard feelings, and utter disregard for his feelings and welfare.

This final effort of closing and seeking a confession is important to the case and important to you if you do it right. It leaves in the mind of the suspect several important suggestions. First, that he can communicate with you later if he wants to, and second, that you do not believe him and would like to see him get himself straightened out. This is important because the suspect must believe that you do not believe him. If he feels that he has convinced you of his innocence, that will make it easier for him to resist you later, or even convince someone else of his innocence. Further, if this suspect has any kind of conscience, it will work on him and it just might be that he will call you later on his own volition with the confession.

You should insert this effort in the conclusion of every unsuccessful interrogation. However, this final seeking for confession must be done tactfully. Certainly, every interrogation will bring about a different set of circumstances, and you must use these to fit the situation. The suggestions I make are only ideas of and examples of what I mean, for you should fit your own case to the idea and use your own words in this effort. But I do suggest that you should always try once more for a confession when you have decided to close out your interrogation effort.

When you conclude your interrogation effort, never lock the door to any further contacts with the person. Being angry and hollering has this effect. By leaving an opening to renew your conversation with the person, you do not alienate him, and you do not put yourself beyond his reach. Sometimes, a suspect will want just a little time to think over all of the things that you have said to him, and then may decide that, sure enough, the right thing to do is confess. If the subject is left knowing that you are open to contact should he want to talk to you, he may make the effort to contact you and even give you his subsequent confession. Never ever put yourself out on a limb and cut yourself off from your suspect in the parting shots. Everybody loses if you do this, including the victim, yourself, your department, law and order, and most of all, the subject, by not being able to get his troubles straightened out with someone he trusts and respects. As before, let me offer a few samples of what I have in mind for this kind of "closing with the door open":

Interrogator: "Karl, I want you to know that I don't feel that this whole problem has been straightened out. I want you to think things over and we can get together later, and maybe go over this whole thing again."

or

Interrogator: "Karl, why don't you kick this thing around in your mind awhile and think over what we have been talking about. All you have to do is let your conscience be your guide in all of this, and then, if you need me to talk over anything, just give a whistle."

or

Interrogator: "Look, Karl, I am not going to try and con you into anything. All I want you to do is apply some logic to what we have been talking about and when you do, I feel that you will give me a call and we can get things straightened out."

In all phases of your interrogation, you must make yourself available to receive the confession, and this holds true at the termination of the interrogation as well. By leaving yourself and the suspect an opening to renew your conversation, you'll quite often give yourself a confession that you would not otherwise have gotten. Make yourself available to the suspect and give yourself the break of being able to easily renew any further contact you might have with him.

To sum up this portion, let's make a list of why we should pursue this open type of closing.

1. You might have to talk to the suspect again, either about this case or maybe about something in the future.

2. Some other interrogator might have to work with him and you would not have alienated him to further police efforts.

3. You have left yourself "available" to him for further contacts should he decide to come in with his admission.

4. You would never have to make excuses in a court of law and try to explain away any embarrassing behavior on your part. You could show continued interest in the subject's welfare throughout your whole contact with him.

The above list gives just a few reasons for my suggestion of a "soft"-type closing. Many more could be included here, but the above list is sufficient to point out a few of the many reasons for this recommended "open"-type closing.

Now, let's check back with our case and see how it has progressed and how it fits in with these ideas. When we left the case, the interrogator was just beginning to employ the more refined interrogation techniques to this person. As was previously suggested, you should read other interrogation books for the purpose of obtaining these more advanced methods. My effort here is to give you the basic foundation of this interrogation business so that you can add to your own ability and capability through the use of more technical and advanced effort in addition to this solid foundation.

Therefore, the central part of the conversation in our case will not be included here as it will employ these previously mentioned techniques. All interrogation is keyed toward the end result of a confession. The more that you read about interrogation, the better you will be able to use the subtle urgings and refined psychological stimuli with your suspect. A good interrogator is well versed in many methods of obtaining confessions, and only through study and experimentation will one ever develop a number of methods for approaching a subject. Further, only by a basic understanding of interrogation and your relationship with the subject can you ever build a successful and usable arsenal of adequate interrogation methods. Don't ever be lulled into finding one method that works occasionally and then never trying anything else. Diversification is what keeps a business healthy, and diversification is what makes an interrogator's reputation for excellence.

In our case, our interrogator has reached a point at which he has tried the "one more time" routine without success and he has, therefore, decided to conclude the interrogation for the present. The suspect has denied everything throughout, and he has, at this time, been told exactly what the offense was, what he is suspected of, and why.

Suspect: "I don't know anything about what happened at Sam's. I said already that I left and went to Kelly's house and slept there. I came back to town, looked in Sam's, then went to Jackie and Len's, ate, and then went home to bed."

Interrogator: "I know what you've said, Karl, but we still have this case on our hands and, further, we have a witness that saw you carry a box from the bar this morning."

Suspect: "I swear to you that I didn't carry any box out of Sam's Place this morning. I looked in, and when I didn't see anyone there, I left. Whoever said they saw me leaving there with a box is lying, 'cause I didn't carry any box from there. If I would have had a box, somebody else on the street would have said so too. I didn't break in there and that's all there is to it."

Interrogator: "You know, we've been talking here quite awhile, and all along, throughout the whole conversation, Karl, I've had this feeling that you're holding out on me. I know that it's tough to admit a mistake, and I also know that it takes a better man to stand up and say that he did something wrong than to act like a kid when trouble comes along and pretend in your mind it didn't happen. I wish that you'd look at this problem in this light and go ahead and get it off your chest. I can't get you out of trouble, you know that, but once this problem is out in the open and we discuss it you will see things in a much clearer light. I believe that a person should tell the truth at all times, and I feel that you should go ahead and tell me all about anything that we haven't discussed today. I don't think that you're the kind of man that can live with a lie comfortably, so why don't you go on and tell me all about it now."

Suspect: "I already told you all I know; I can't tell you any more."

Interrogator: "I'll tell you what I'd like for you to do, Karl. I want you to think over what we've discussed today and also what you know you should do about it. You come from a fine home, and your parents are fine people. You know they'd tell you to tell the truth about anything that you got yourself into. I would hate to see you get yourself in trouble and then make another mistake by lying about it. I believe that you're the kind of guy who can tell the truth if you'll just let yourself. I want you to think this thing over for awhile and I believe that you'll see that I've been telling you the truth. If you want to talk to me again, all you have to do is ask. If there is any question that comes to your mind, just come and see me, and I'll give you an answer if I can. Think it over for awhile, Karl, and I'm sure we can get it straightened out the next time we talk, OK?"

Suspect: "OK."

So, we've gotten our case to the point where we could go no further without wearing both the subject and the interrogator out. But, as you noticed, we left ourselves plenty of room to start anew at a later date if necessary, and also we made our interrogator "available" should the suspect feel that he wants to talk. We tried for the confession and thereby reinforced in the suspect's mind the fact that we are not convinced that he is innocent as he has stated; further, we gave him a number of good reasons to think about as to why he should confess. By leaving the door open to him, we can renew our conversation anytime by just saying, "Well, Karl, did you think over what we talked about last time?" Further, this termination of our interrogation will give the investigating officers more time to check further in the case and maybe produce the witness. Long, drawn-out interrogations are never acceptable, so the interrogator must decide when his subject has had enough and then gracefully and professionally withdraw. His manner in terminating the interrogation is very important, and I sincerely suggest this "open door" type of closing.

Chapter 9

REDUCING IT TO WRITING

AT PRESENT, there is a great deal of concern and interest in this act of taking a statement. Recent Supreme Court decisions have affected and somewhat upset many long-standing ideas and conceptions of just what to do and how to take a statement in order for that statement to be acceptable in our courts.

All of the decisions so far have been based on mistakes made in the case itself, but the concern, I feel, is about the trend of the opinions being handed down. There is not now, and never has been, any excuse for a poorly or improperly taken statement. Nothing excuses an officer or official if he has taken an illegal statement. I think that these decisions serve only to remind us, the interrogators, that we must always be diligent and correct in something as ultimately important as a statement. Never forget that what we do will have some effect on someone else's life, and he in turn will affect other people's lives. As guardians of our citizens' liberty and freedom, we must always be right and must always diligently avoid making any mistakes in our work.

Statement taking is the summation of our interrogation effort. Once the admission has been orally made, we must continue the effort until the person involved has reduced his admission to written words and has signed it before acceptable and unbiased witnesses. A statement, in and of itself, is not enough to prove anyone guilty or innocent of a charge. Statements always have to be proven by facts and other evidence in a case. A statement, however, does support your case and serves as a guideline for your investigation effort. Further, it supports the facts that you have gathered and will, in essence, be the summation of your fact gathering by telling its story of the case at hand. A statement serves as an adhesive for your physical evidence as well as circumstantial evidence because it will bind all of the details previously submitted into one short, understandable unit written in the words of the suspect. A statement is a most desirable piece of evidence and in almost every case, you should attempt to obtain a voluntary, freely given statement from the subject.

CONTENTS

First, let's consider what a statement should contain. In a recent discussion I had with a criminal court judge, this point was brought up and I inquired into what he thought was the most usable type of statement as far as its contents were concerned.

He said that a statement should be a short, concise synopsis of the events of the crime and should not be a rambling-type form. A statement does not need to hammer away at each minute detail. A capsule recapitulation of the entire incident is the most desirable. If the subject begins to ramble during the statement and it is read to a jury, it will be extremely hard to concentrate on and the jury will soon lose the gist of the content. If the story is brief, to the point, and contains just the high points of the event, then after just a short reading, any jury will have had made available to them the meat of the crime in the subject's own words and will not have been loaded up with a lot of superfluous words. Always avoid wordiness in your statements. No judge or jury in the world will be impressed with your ability to make up and deliver long, involved questions. Ordinarily, they are not interested, at least as far as the statement is concerned, in what the subject did prior to or after any given situation.

A statement should have the same effect as a single arrow. It should go straight to the target and hit it right in the middle. All of the other facts and necessities in a case can be brought out during testimony from the stand, but a statement of the facts in a short, concise form will have a far more dramatic effect than some book length recapitulation of the entire case.

It is best to try and limit yourself to one-page statements. In this manner, you can avoid getting too wordy and also you can keep your questions more closely centered on the issue at hand. By knowing that you are limited in the space you have available, you are not so inclined to go rambling off into left field. Everything will be kept "cued" in on the issue at hand and getting it down in a short, concise form. This is not to say that a one-page statement is a hard and fast rule. Occasionally, you will need more space, but using this rule as a guideline will help you gauge the amount of space available. It goes without saying that everything a subject says during the taking of this statement must be put down in the exact words he uses. This, in itself, will cause the length to vary, but by adroit questioning you can keep your questions short and right to the point.

Never plunge into a statement without first considering what you want this statement to reflect. It will only say what you bring out by your questioning. The statement, like the entire interrogation, deserves some preplanning consideration. Consider the issue—what the subject has orally admitted and how to best cover the heart of his story in a short, briefly told review.

TYPE

In my opinion, a "question and answer" type statement is far superior to a long "narrative" type. A narrative-type statement tends to ramble and become overly long and involved, and there is always the suspicion of "coaching" by the interrogator, especially if the subject is mentally dull. Never say anything during a statement-taking session that you do not want put down in just the manner that you say it. Side comments or suggestions are certainly wrong and you should expect everything spoken to be on the written record. It is well to imagine that a tape recorder is turned on during the entire session, for this will prevent you from becoming involved in any side suggestions or comments.

The "question and answer" type statement is shorter and can be brought more directly to the point. Further, if some defense attorney in court strikes out some portion, there will still be some usable portions left, whereas in a "narrative" statement, nothing remains. Keep your questions short and to the point, and most often the suspect will do the same thing. Never lead your suspect, but allow him to tell the story. Never put words in his mouth by suggesting he committed a crime and identifying the crime itself. Let him tell what he did and how he did it—you just guide the conversation. It is far better to say, "What did you do on August 12, John?" than to say, "Tell me about that robbery you pulled on August 12th, John." The first questioner inquires, but allows the suspect to tell the story, while the second accuses him of the act with an extremely leading question. Never allow any of your questions to accuse your suspect of this or any other crime. Let him make his admissions in his own manner. You do not need to accuse him of anything. There is an old salesman's adage: "Never ask a question that can be answered with just a Yes or No." Compose your questions so that they will require some explanation from your suspect, and you will capture the flavor of his story. His answering just Yes or No puts you in a defensive position when you want to be in a neutral position on the statement. It is better to say, "What did you do on August 12th, John?" than it is to say, "Did you do something wrong on August 12th, John?" The first question invites explanation and the second question invites the answer Yes to which you must then ask, "Tell me about it, will you?" By avoiding single-word answers, you not only shorten your questions but you reduce the number of questions you must ask. The more you have to say on a statement, the more chance for error there is on your part.

In the body of your statement, make all of your answers center around the admission of the act itself. Usually, when a person is giving a statement, he will admit the offense during the first few questions. This is fine, but you must direct your questions so that they will repeat this admission in some other part of the questioning procedure. Thus, if one part of the statement is struck from the record, then the admission by the subject still remains as part of your total effort. After the opening (which will be discussed later), you usually will ask some type of neutral question that will cause the subject to respond by making his admission of committing the crime. If you sit quietly for just a few seconds, he will usually tell the whole story in a few short sentences. Then, you can cover anything he left out with a few short questions following the admission. Try to get the admission of the act in at least two different places in the statement prior to the closing statement. I feel that both the opening statement and the closing statement in the body of the confession serves an extremely important purpose and you must consider them both very carefully. Both of these points will be discussed at some length, but they should not be confused with the body of the statement. In the body of the confession, you want a short admission in at least two places with everything that is said having a direct bearing on the issue at hand.

OPENING STATEMENT

The "opening of the statement" must not be confused with the "heading of the statement." The "heading" is a coached portion that precedes the actual statement itself and is usually predesigned by your department. The "opening statement" is contained in the body of the statement itself and is spoken within the statement-taking session and is taken down by the recorder or stenographer and reduced to writing. The opening serves as an "announcement of intention and purpose" for your efforts which follow. Above all, you must never, during the announcement, accuse the subject of anything. What you tell him is exactly what you are doing and who you are. You remind him of certain rights so that anything that follows appears as his voluntary statement. If you tell him ahead of time what you are doing and that he does not have to cooperate, and he does cooperate, it makes his efforts acceptable in the eyes of the court and certainly any jury he goes before. As an example, an opening might go something like this: "John, as you know, I am Sgt. Starr and this is Mrs. Hurst, our secretary. I have asked Mrs. Hurst to come in and record our conversation and later she will reduce it to writing and we can look it over at that time. If you recall, before we began talking, I advised you of your constitutional rights and you initialed the card. Remember that you have a right to remain silent and anything you say will be used in court as evidence against you; you are entitled to talk to an attorney now and have him present now or at any time during questioning. If you cannot afford an attorney, one will be appointed for you without cost, plus you must understand all of these rights that are yours. You have stated to me that you would like to give me a statement about some of your actions and this is what our conversation will concern itself with. You know you do not have to, so if you wish to continue, why don't you start by telling me what you did on August 12th of this year?"

This opening can be altered in many ways to fit your circumstances, but you should always include something of its kind in the beginning of your statements. You let him know where he stands, and then the statement is that much more voluntary if he proceeds. If he objects or refuses at this time, he would probably refute any statement you would have gotten anyway. It serves no useful purpose to get a weak or poorly taken statement from a subject, as it will more than likely be denied admission in court. If the statement you obtain is fair and proper and you have taken every safeguard for yourself and your subject's protection, then the likelihood of court admission is inherent. By using this kind of opening announcement of purpose and intent, you have taken yet another step in safeguarding your suspect's guaranteed rights and leaving the decision of waiving them directly within his control. All of the favorite defense tactics grow a little dim if you give your suspect all of the benefits and go far enough to put them down in the body of the statement so there can be no mistake of your desire to remain neutral in your efforts.

CLOSING STATEMENT

Another method which supports the voluntary nature of the statement is to ask one or two more questions, following the final question concerning the crime, that have no direct bearing on the case, but which do call for volunteered answers from the subject. Something like the following is suggested:

Q. "What kind of work does your father do, John?"

or

Q. "Where did you stay when you first came into town, John?"

or

Q. "Where do your parents live at this time, John?"

These kinds of questions, answered by the subject, will prove beyond a reasonable doubt that during the time the statement was being given, the subject was freely and voluntarily furnishing information. This kind of voluntary information has no bearing on the case, but it is helpful in that it shows that you were not forcing the person to give information. It indicates that he was answering freely and giving information that was available only from his mind. There is no need to hammer away at these questions, but by the insertion of this kind of question at the end, you can then assume that all the preceding information was just as freely given. Always try to ask the question

   Q. "Have you been promised anything or offered any reward to give this statement?"

This question will have a tendency to prove that the subject is freely and voluntarily cooperating with you if his answer is No. If he answers Yes, you would be sunk in court anyway, but the No answer serves to bolster the statement. It becomes more difficult for him later to say that he was offered all kinds of inducements if, at the time of the statement taking, you ask him how he feels about giving the statement and he states that he is giving it without inducements of any kind. The first thing that you run into in court is the argument that you offered him all manner of promises in order to extract the confession. If you answer this charge during the original statement-taking session, you weaken any accusation of this kind that comes up later.

   Finally, ask a person the following:

   Q. "Is there anything else you would like to add to this statement?"

This question serves to conclude the question-asking period and shows that the statement has ended. His opinion, at this point in the statement, will help support his previously spoken words and it will also allow your subject to express any final opinion he might have concerning this issue. Don't be afraid of this question, because if he has given the statement freely, he will usually feel remorse and will express regret of the commission of the crime.

TYPING

It is considerably easier to read a typed statement than any other kind. Further, a typed statement makes a far more presentable package because it is clear and clean and everyone who can read will be able to understand what is written there. Occasionally, you will obtain a handwritten statement. This is good, as it further proves the voluntariness of the statement itself. The only problem with a handwritten statement is that occasionally they are extremely hard to read. All of us have a different handwriting, and some of us practically scrawl what we attempt to write. If a handwritten statement is poorly written, it will be very difficult to decipher by the time it gets to court. On the other hand, a typewritten statement will remain clear and anyone will be able to read what is written there. It is my suggestion that wherever possible, one should try and reduce an oral admission to a typewritten statement for preservation. There are a few rules that you should follow during this typing that will remain constant throughout all statements that you take.

Immediately preceding your first question, type the following in capital letters:

STATEMENT   TIME NOW IS_____A.M. This gives a definite boundary to the statement and indicates that everything following this remark is the actual language used in the question and answering session following. The time also proves just how long the session took and will indicate whether it was a long grilling session or a short, properly considerate session. Following the final question, again the words, STATEMENT   TIME NOW IS_____A.M., are used. This closes off the question and answer part and shows exactly when and where the questioning was concluded.

There should be no double-spacing in a statement, as that can suggest room for putting in more words after the statement is signed by the subject. By single-spacing and keeping everything together, you remove the accusation of having added something later. This accusation (like promises) is a favorite method of discrediting statements in court.

In the body of the statement, each question should be preceded by the letter "Q," and then the question should be written out in full wordage. The subject's answer should be preceded by the letter "A," and then his full answer should be written out. By identifying them in this method, there is no mistake as to who said what during the questioning period and it is also quite clear what part each took. Again, no double-spaces should appear. Each answer should be written directly below the question.

Let's put this together and see what the form should look like.

STATEMENT   THE TIME IS 9:05 A.M.

Q.
A.
Q.
A.
Q.

A.

Q. Is there anything you would like to add?

A. Nothing other than I wish I hadn't broken in.

STATEMENT END   THE TIME IS 9:08 A.M.

In this form, everything is complete and gives the appearance of a neat package to which nothing could be added or left out.

It is often said that a deliberate typographical error is advantageous in the body of a statement, as you can have the subject initial the mistake to prove that he read the entire statement before he signed it. I subscribe to this idea as long as it is not overdone. I have seen some statements that, following this treatment, appear as if they were handwritten or else as if the person doing the typing was very inept. You want it to appear official and intelligent, not as if some beginning typing student hacked his way through it. Choosing one or two spots and making typing errors serves as a useful tool to show that the suspect read it. If many more than one or two errors appear, you must spend a needlessly long time having each one initialed. It is the obligation of the person taking the statement to have each error and each typing mistake corrected and initialed by the subject in ink before he signs the statement itself. Everything on the statement must be just right before it is signed; once it is signed, nothing must be changed or altered. Use discretion in your mistake-making, and you will have proof of the subject's reading of the statement as well as a much more presentable statement.

Make sure all the words spoken are put down in the order they were spoken. Never omit profanity if the subject used profanity. Never try to correct the subject's English, regardless of how good or bad it is. Never suggest words to him that he may not know the meaning of. Put down exactly what he says and put down exactly what you say. Nothing more but most certainly nothing less. If you are constant in your demand for using the exact words and phrases of you and your subject, you will never have to defend yourself in court when accused of changing a statement. If you omit profanity, correct English, correct pronunciation, and so on, you have, in effect, changed the statement; technically, the statement is useless. Put it down exactly and you will have a usable statement.

HEADING

Usually, there is a printed or typed announcement preceding the actual statement itself. The wording in this announcement is as varied as there are statement-takers, and I am not going to say which is right and which is wrong. This "heading" should be on every statement, as it serves as an identification tag of the place, date, action, and those present at the time. It also serves to advise the subject of his rights and reminds him of what he is doing and what can happen. I will insert the heading that I use, but this in no way is a suggestion that it is the only acceptable heading; you can contact your local legal official, solicitor, district attorney, city attorney, or the like and ask him what wording he considers to be the best in your area.

This heading should be set aside and should precede the body of the statement itself. It should never appear to be part of the question and answer part of the statement and should only appear to be the "form" that precedes the questioning itself. Usually, the wording in this "heading" is formal. In the case of low-IQ subjects, it will appear to be foreign to most vocabularies. It is best to set this "heading" apart from the body of the statement so you cannot be accused of putting words in the subject's mouth or adding something unknown or unspoken by the subject.

I believe that it would be a distinct advantage to have this heading printed by a professional printer on stationery that could be used for statement taking only.

If you type out the heading on plain stationery, be sure and separate the heading from the statement itself. If you are asked in court if this is part of the statement, always say that this was put on the document as it was being typed and is not part of the question and answer part of the statement. If you attempt to include it in the question and answer procedure itself, more than likely, the accused will refute the entire statement by stating that the heading was not part of the question and answer period.

This heading is a rather formal statement of facts. It contains information that is important to have the subject acquainted with but not usually brought out during the statement-taking session itself. In every case, the heading is read by the subject prior to his signing the confession, but this is after the admission has been reduced to writing. The wording used in this heading is left up to the discretion of the user, but in order to more effectively explain what I am talking about, I will insert the heading that I presently use.

I, ———, age ———, address ——— am aware that I am under arrest for ———. I have been advised and had explained to me prior to answering any questions, either oral or written, that I have the right to remain silent; that anything I say will be used in court as evidence against me; that I am entitled to talk to an attorney now, and have him present now or at any time during questioning; that if I cannot afford an attorney, one will be appointed for me without cost; and that I understand these rights.

I, ———, do hereby make the following statement, voluntarily and of my own free will, without fear or compulsion and without inducements or promises of leniency, after having been warned of my constitutional rights, and with the knowledge that any statement I make may be used as evidence against me before the court or jury. I am aware that I have the right to remain silent and not bear witness against myself as guaranteed by the Constitution of the United States. Statement taken in the Criminal Investigation Bureau of the ——— Police Dept. on ———, in the presence of ——— and ———, of the ——— Police Dept.
BEGINNING OF STATEMENT: TIME IS NOW:

All of the above information can be repeated in the first question if you so desire, and occasionally, it is a good idea to do so. However, the heading is not meant to be the first question. It is the announcement of who is there, what is happening, when, and what the suspect is doing.

Be sure and have your subject read every word on this heading before he signs the confession. You will notice that there are some parts of it that require specific knowledge of the case and subject at hand. It pays to have the subject himself fill in these spots in his own handwriting. Further, it is good to have your suspect initial the middle of this heading to prove that it was there at the time the statement was written. You must always protect yourself from accusations of having added something later, and the best way to do this is to have the suspect initial or sign his name on each part of the statement. It also pays to ask the suspect if he understands what this heading means before you proceed into reading the statement.

You can restate it so that he understands the contents, and he then cannot come back with the remark that he did not know what he was doing. The heading makes it very clear just what he is doing, and if you make it clear in his mind, there can be no question in his mind what is going on.

"I HAVE READ" CLOSING

The final thing that is put on the typed statement is the final sentence: I HAVE READ OR HAVE HAD READ THE ABOVE STATEMENT AND FIND IT TRUE AND CORRECT TO THE BEST OF MY KNOWLEDGE AND BELIEF. This sentence is placed on the statement face below the final word "STATEMENT," and is used to show that the person has, in fact, read it. It indicates that what is written there is true and in his own words. If you are positive that the person giving the statement can read, you can omit the words, "HAVE HAD READ," but if you or someone else reads it to him be sure and signify that this was the case. Also, identify the person that read the statement by having him indicate next to his signature that he read it to the suspect. After the suspect has read the entire statement including this final statement, you ask him if this is true and correct to the best of his ability and belief and then state that if this is the case, "would you please sign this statement."

SUBJECT SIGNATURE AND WITNESS SIGNATURE

After the suspect has read the entire statement, has corrected the mistakes and initialed them, has initialed all of the typing errors, and has been asked if the statement is true and correct, he is then asked to sign it. This signature is handwritten by him and he is asked to sign his usual signature. The spot for his signature is below the "I Have Read" closing and on the right-hand start of the page. It usually appears as follows:

John Jacob Doe
March 3, 1971

The whole name is typed in below the line in order to remove any doubt as to who is giving the statement. Also, the date is placed just below the name in order to reaffirm the exact date of the signing. It is not important that the person signing the statement put down his whole name. He can write out his name if he desires, but his usual signature is sufficient and often is better since samples of this signature can be obtained in other places for comparison should the need arise to prove that he, in fact, signed it. The signature should always be written out in pen and ink.

Below the signature line and on the left-hand side of the page, the word "WITNESSES" is typed in. Immediately below this word, several lines are typed in for the signatures of those persons witnessing the signing of the statement. Any adult person can be a witness to the subject's signature. The more witnesses you have, the better prepared you will be if later you are accused of forcing the signature. They can testify to the appearance of the suspect plus the fact that they saw him voluntarily sign his name. Always make sure that your witnesses actually see the signing and then make sure that they sign their names in the presence of the suspect. The WITNESS block will appear as follows:

WITNESSES

_____ ___

_____

_____

As in the case of the subject's signature, the witnesses signature should be their usual signature. They should be legible and should be written in pen and ink. Titles are not important, but can be placed there if the witnesses so desire. If the first witness has read the statement to the suspect, he should include this fact immediately following his name by using some short phrase such as "read by" or something similar. I have always made it a practice that if I do the questioning in the statement, I sign the first witness blank. In this manner, I can always identify a statement that I took regardless of how much later it is used. Whoever does the actual questioning should always sign first.

In the case of a statement running more than one page, you must concern yourself with one additional signature. In the case of more than one page, you should have your subject sign diagonally from the lower left corner of the page toward the upper right-hand corner. Have him sign in a bold hand so that his signature covers most of the page. In this manner, it indicates that all of the typing was on the page when the signature was affixed. The witnesses' signatures should appear on each page of the statement in the same general location as on the last page. Usually, there is no set location for the witnesses' signatures on the first page of more than one-page statements, but the witnesses should still sign in the lower left-hand corner.

In the case of a two or more page statement, the typist should identify the pages as follows:

PAGE ONE OF A TWO-PAGE STATEMENT
then
PAGE TWO OF A TWO-PAGE STATEMENT

If the statement has more pages, then each page should be identified as shown above and placed in its proper sequence. This identification of the page numbers should appear on the bottom of the first page and in the upper left-hand corner of each succeeding page.

A note from our suspect will let us see what a statement looks like, in total, as it pertains to our case.

FIGURE 10

NOTE TO M. STAR

To: Marshall Star, Criminal Investigation Bureau
From: J.F., Desk
Subject: Karl Clayton
Clayton wants to talk to you as soon as you can make it.

FIGURE 11

ORLANDO POLICE DEPARTMENT

I, ——————, age ———, address ————— am aware that I am under arrest for ——————————. I have been advised and had explained to me prior to answering any questions, either oral or written, that I have the right to remain silent; that anything I say will be used in court as evidence against me; that I am entitled to talk to an attorney now, and have him present now or at any time during questioning; that if I cannot afford an attorney, one will be appointed for me without cost; and that I understand these rights.

I, ———————————————, do hereby make the following statement, voluntarily, and of my own free will, without fear or compulsion and without inducements or promises of leniency, after having been warned of my constitutional rights, and with the knowledge that any statement I make may be used as evidence against me before the court or jury. I am aware that I have the right to remain silent and not bear witness against myself as guaranteed by the Constitution of the United States.

Statement taken in the Criminal Investigation Bureau of the Orlando Police Department on ——————— in the presence of ——————————— and — — — ——————————— of the Orlando Police Department, and ———————, Secretary, Criminal Investigation Bureau.

TIME IS NOW: 9:10 A. M., BEGINNING OF STATEMENT

Q.
A.
Q.
A.
Q.
A.
Q.
A.
Q.
A.
Q.
A.
Q.
A.
Q.
A.
Q.
A.
Q.
A.
Q. John, is there anything else you would like to add?
A. No.

END OF STATEMENT, TIME IS NOW 9:16 A.M.

I have read the foregoing statement or confession, or have had the foregoing statement or confession read to me by ——————————— of the Orlando Police Department, and I find it to be true, accurate and correct, to the best of my ability and knowledge. I have initialed each of the ——— foregoing pages and willingly affix my signature to this last page, No. ———.

JOHN JACOB DOE

Witness

Witness

Interrogator: "Karl, I got your word that you wanted to talk to me."

Suspect: "Yes, Sir. I had a talk with my father and I want to get this thing off of my chest."

Interrogator: "Are you trying to tell me that you broke into Sam's Place?"

Suspect: "I didn't break in but I did steal the stuff from there."

Interrogator: "Suppose you take it from the beginning and tell me just what happened step by step, Karl."

Suspect: "Well, I went uptown just like I said and I went into Sam's just like I told you before. But when I was in Sam's I got too much to drink and I went to sleep in one of the booths in the back. I guess they locked up without seeing me because when I woke up it was early morning and nobody was there. I got up and looked around and couldn't find anybody there. I didn't have no idea to steal nothing but when I didn't find anybody there I decided to take the cigarettes and records. I got one of the tablecloths and put all of the stuff in it and carried it outside with me. I wasn't lying when I said I didn't have no box when I left there. I had the stuff in a tablecloth."

Interrogator: "Did you see anyone when you left there?"

Suspect: "Yes, Sir. I saw this guy, I don't know his name, and I told him that I was cleaning up for Sam."

Interrogator: "When you left the place, where did you go then?"

Suspect: "I put the bag of stuff behind the warehouse, under the loading platform and then went to the restaurant like I figured I would wait awhile before I tried to take the stuff home so I wouldn't be so noticeable. I got a box at the restaurant and went back and put the stuff in it and got on the bus and took it home.

Interrogator: "Where are the cigarettes and records at now, Karl?"

Suspect: "They're stuffed way up under the house. I couldn't take them in the house 'cause Ma would see them and want to know where they came from. If you go on the west side of the house and look up near where the chimney is, you'll see the box. All the stuff is still there, I didn't use any of it."

Interrogator: "Where is the tablecloth that you used to remove the items from Sam's Place?"

Suspect: "I threw it back under the loading platform."

Interrogator: "How did you get out of Sam's Place, Karl? Did you have to break out?"

Suspect: "No. They have a night lock on the inside. I just turned the handle and walked out. I left the door open when I left. I didn't tear up anything inside either. All of the stuff, the cigarette machine and the juke, was standing open when I was looking around inside. I probably wouldn't have taken anything if they had been closed."

Now that we have the confession, the proper thing to do is to pursue the case to its proper end and get the confession down on paper.

Interrogator: "Karl, would you give me a written statement concerning these things you have just told me?"

Suspect: "Yes, Sir. I want to get it straightened out."

Interrogator: "While I get the stenographer, do you want to call anyone? You know you have the right to call anyone you like."

Suspect: "No, Sir. I don't want to call anyone."

At this point, the investigators and the secretary should be invited into the room. All of these people can later testify as to the subject's condition and also to what was said and done during the statement-taking session.

Interrogator: "Karl, I have asked these people in to witness this statement and I will introduce them to you in just a minute. I will remind you that you don't have to give this statement. If you wish to continue with it, just say so and we will go ahead."

Suspect: "Yes, Sir. I want to go ahead."

Interrogator: "Karl, as you know, my name is Marshall Starr and this is Sgt. Weiderhold and Sgt. Smith. This is Mrs. Hurst and she will take down everything we say in shorthand and later put it in writing. I must warn you that this statement can be used in court, and I must also remind you that you can call an attorney before you give me this statement, if you wish. If you do want to continue, why don't you tell me what you did on the evening of May 19, 1971."

Suspect: "Well, I went to Sam's Place after supper and had some drinks. I went to sleep in there and when I woke up, everybody was gone so I got up and looked around and then put some cigarettes in a tablecloth and got some records and put them in there too. I carried this stuff over behind the warehouse and later took it home."

Interrogator: "How did you get in Sam's Place, Karl?"

Suspect: "I went in when it was open. I had some drinks and then went to sleep in a booth."

Interrogator: "How did you leave?"

Suspect: "I just opened the night lock and walked out."

Interrogator: "You mentioned carrying something out of Sam's. What was this and what happened to it?"

Suspect: "I took a bunch of cigarettes and some records from the juke. I took these things first to over behind the warehouse, then I put them in a box and took them home. I put the box under my house and I guess it is still there. I didn't use any of the stuff I took, I just took it home and hid it under the house."

Interrogator: "How old are you, Karl, and where were you born?"

Suspect: "I'm 23 years old and I was born at Baker's Hospital in Charleston, South Carolina."

Interrogator: "Have you been made any promises or offered any deals or inducements to give this statement, Karl?"

Suspect: "No, Sir."

Interrogator: "Is there anything you would like to add to this statement?"

Suspect: "I know that I did the wrong thing to steal that stuff from Sam's. I want to get it straightened out, that's all."

So now we have the whole story down on paper and ready to be transcribed and written up. We have included just the highlights of the incident in the statement in order not to get wordy. We have tried to capture the incident in capsule form and have left the proof of the incident to the investigators. Physical evidence is an absolute necessity in every case and a statement should never be substituted for physical or other evidence in a case.

After the statement is prepared, the suspect must read every word aloud and then initial mistakes. He must understand everything that is there and then verbally agree that it is all true and correct to the best of his ability and belief. After all of this is done, he will be asked to sign the statement.

I have included the signed statement in Figure 12. This statement completes the job of the interrogator. The rest of the case is then routine investigation.

FIGURE 12

ORLANDO POLICE DEPARTMENT

I, —————, age ——, address ————— am aware that I am under arrest for ———————————. I have been advised and had explained to me prior to answering any questions, either oral or written, that I have the right to remain silent; that anything I say will be used in court as evidence against me; that I am entitled to talk to an attorney now, and have him present now or at any time during questioning; that if I cannot afford an attorney, one will be appointed for me without cost; and that I understand these rights.

I, ——————————————, do hereby make the following statement, voluntarily, and of my own free will, without fear or compulsion and without inducements or promises of leniency, after having been warned of my constitutional rights, and with the knowledge that any statement I make may be used as evidence against me before the court or jury. I am aware that I have the right to remain silent and not bear witness against myself as guaranteed by the Constitution of the United States.

Statement taken in the Criminal Investigation Bureau of the Orlando Police Department on ————— in the presence of Marshall Starr and Sgt. Wiederhold of the Orlando Police Department, and Mrs. Hurst, Secretary, Criminal Investigation Bureau.

TIME IS NOW: 9:10 A.M., BEGINNING OF STATEMENT

Q. Karl, as you know, my name is Marshall Starr and this is Sgt. Wiederhold and Sgt. Smith. This is Mrs. Hurst, and she will take down everything we say in shorthand and later put it in writing. I must warn you that this statement can be used in court and I must also remind you that you can call an attorney before you give me this statement, if you wish. If you want to continue, why don't you tell me what you did on the evening of May 21, 1971.

A. Well, I went to Sam's Place after supper and had some drinks. I went to sleep in there and when I woke up everybody was gone, so I got up, and looked around and then put some cigarettes in a tablecloth and got some records and put them in there too. I carried this stuff over behind the warehouse and later took it home.

Q. How did you get in Sam's Place, Karl?

A. I went in when it was open. I had some drinks and then went to sleep in a booth.

Q. How did you leave?

A. I just opened the night lock and walked out.

Q. You mentioned carrying something out of Sam's. What was this and what happened to it?

A. I took a bunch of cigarettes and some records from the juke. I took these things first to over behind the warehouse, and then I put them in a box and took them home. I put the box under my house and I guess it is still there. I didn't use any of the stuff I took. I just took it home and hid it under the house.

Q. How old are you, Karl, and where were you born?

A. I'm 23 years old and I was born at Baker's Hospital in Charleston, South Carolina.

Q. Have you been made any promises or offered any deals or inducements to give this statement, Karl?

A. No sir.

Q. Is there anything you would like to add to this statement?

A. I know that I did the wrong thing to steal that stuff from Sam's. I want to get it straightened out, that's all.

END OF STATEMENT, TIME IS NOW: 9:15 A.M.

I have read the foregoing statement or confession, or have had the foregoing statement or confession read to me by ——————————— of the Orlando Police Department, and I find it to be true, accurate and correct, to the best of my ability and knowledge. I have initialed each of the ————— foregoing pages and willingly affix my signature to this last page, No. —————.

KARL CLAYTON

Witness

Witness

Chapter 10

YOU, THE INTERROGATOR

Now that we have the words, let's put the interrogator himself in the fishbowl, and see what makes for a good appearance and successful image. Nothing is more important than your words; however, they have to come from the proper setting. In our case, the interrogator must have the proper appearance and delivery in order to present the words effectively. We have talked throughout this entire book about professionalization and certainly, physical appearance plays a very important part in this image. The way you look and the expression and connotation given to the words you use will sell just as much as what the words say. Professionalization is not just a word; it is an attitude that you must adopt and an image that you must present in order to carry out the whole theme of being a professional interrogator.

CLOTHES

The basic requirement for proper appearance is a coat, necktie, and a dress shirt. When so dressed, you certainly appear much better in the subject's eyes. If you enter the room with a neat, businesslike appearance, you immediately radiate a businesslike attitude. On the other hand, if you go into an interrogation situation dressed no better than the subject, it certainly does not give a very good impression. If you do not dress better than the subject, there is nothing about you that will earn his first-impression respect until you begin to verbally sell yourself. If you were to walk into any professional man's office and he were to greet you in a T-shirt and work pants, you would think he had lost his mind. The same is true in the interrogation situation. Do not go in with an open-neck shirt and without a coat or you, too, will be in the position of being ill-prepared for the job at hand. This holds even more true if you have to talk to some businessman or other professional man. You do not look proficient or efficient in anything less than a coat and tie.

Concerning the clothes themselves, the best kind to wear is a conservative or dark-colored suit or coat. Avoid flashy or slick-appearing clothes because anything of this nature is distracting rather than professional-appearing. A dark business-type suit or at least a conservative, dark-colored sport coat is the best. Avoid loud or unusual neckties. Again, anything about your dress that is distracting will not have a positive effect on your subject. All of your dress should appear conservative and radiate a businesslike demeanor. A white shirt is preferable, but a pastel dress shirt is permissible if it is very mild. You should avoid sport shirts worn with a necktie, as it looks very makeshift. In all of your clothes, you want to appear natural and comfortable, not as if you are just putting on an act to impress your subject. I have seen people wearing a necktie which was pulled loose from the neck. Nothing appears more makeshift and sloppy. If you wear the necktie, wear it properly. If you have a coat, wear it, and wear it properly. A lot of people will enter an interrogation room without the coat and with the gun and equipment hanging out. This gives the impression that wearers are flaunting or throwing it up in everyone's face that they are big bad "police." Again, there is no excuse for this kind of conduct or dress. If you have the proper clothes, wear them properly and you will give the proper impression. If you do not have the proper clothes, or are not wearing them properly, you are missing an important advantage over the subject by failing to create a proper image of yourself in his mind.

Avoid the use of flashy jewelry in all cases. The subject is not impressed and occasionally can take a violent opposition to some club pin or group emblem you are wearing. Further, the use of loud or unusual jewelry, tie pins, lapel pins, rings, and so forth, can be distracting when you are trying to keep him thinking of your words. Anything that is unusual or distracting should be avoided.

Whatever you wear, it should be clean and neat and should fit. There is never any excuse for dirty or offensive clothing worn by any interrogator.

APPEARANCE

Always be clean and neat in your appearance. A clean shave and

clean skin is a necessity. You should always have a haircut, prefer-
ably in a neat, clean style. Anything unusual can create a question
in a suspect's mind as to what kind of person you are. The hands
and nails should be clean and trimmed. Dirty hands or dirty nails
are offensive to everyone, and there is no excuse for an interrogator
to appear unkempt in this respect. The subject of personal odor is
a little touchy but should be discussed. There is absolutely no reason
at all for an interrogator to be offensive on this score. Nothing is
more discouraging than to attempt to talk to a person that permeates
the room with offensive body odor. This works on both sides. If
the subject smells, we find it objectionable; likewise, if the interrogator smells, the subject will find that offensive. Carried to any
degree of personal disregard, the interrogation room can become
almost nauseating, and this can be the fault of the interrogator as
well as the subject. Never give anyone reason to find you guilty of
this offensive behavior.

Last of all, you should be meticulous in the case of oral care. Bad
breath is extremely objectionable, and since all you can sell in an
interrogation room is your words, you do not want anything to spoil
your effort. If you are trying to talk quietly and intimately and your
breath keeps causing the suspect to turn away or back up, you never
will be able to create the proper attitude you are striving for. Care
of your teeth is also important, because an unclean mouth is extremely distracting and does nothing to create the impression you
are working towards. All of these suggestions boiled down mean
that you should be neat and clean in your appearance and dress.
There is no excuse for any less than this kind of impression.

POSTURE

Good posture and stance will create a good impression with everyone that you meet. If you walk all slumped over or slouch along,
it can create the impression of weariness on your part or even the
fact that you are not well. If you sit all rolled up in a chair, the
attitude of boredom is created. When you walk, walk alert, briskly,
and radiate the fact that you are wide awake and alert to everything.
When you sit in the interrogation room, sit up straight and relaxed
in your chair with your feet comfortably on the floor, not propped

up on a desk. You want to convey the impression of interest in the subject, and your posture and stance will play an important part in this. If you look alert and wide awake, the subject will believe you are just that. If you look sick, tired, or bored the subject will believe just that. Better the first impression than the last.

FACIAL EXPRESSION

As in all other phases of your interrogation image, your facial expression will have a bearing on the outcome of the interrogation. I am not saying that lack of attention to this point will lose confessions, but I do believe that if you consider this point in your library of tricks, you will obtain more confessions. Excesses must be avoided in any interrogation room. Never overemphasize anything, including your expression. In fact, during the beginning of any conversation, it is best to remove all expression from your face. The person responding to your questions will constantly be scanning your face for some sign, either of approval, belief, disgust, and so on. Whatever he sees there will usually dictate the line of answers he will then follow. If you are smart, you will not show him any of your inner feelings or attitudes by any idle expression. You can suggest anything that you want to by deliberate expression, but avoid giving yourself away by random idle expression.

People are far more interested in talking to an interested listener than to a disinterested or bored listener. As you talk to your subject, concentrate on all that he says and appear to be truly interested in his words. I don't mean that you should stare at him in open wonder, but you should give him the courtesy of your entire attention as long as he is talking. Keeping a sincere and interested look on your face will help your situation a great deal.

As you proceed through your interrogation, if you try to sound upset, look that way. If you tell him how hurt you are by his not telling the truth, appear hurt and slightly put out that he dosen't trust you—not to excess, but enough to add emphasis to your words and other actions. I have always felt that you should concentrate on your subject with only one part of your physical features. If you emphasize some word with a look, then use only your eyes to do it with. Avoid a twitching mouth, waving hands, and any other methods of emphasis. If you involve more than one part, you distract from the total picture. If you use only one part, you can make the emphasis as strong or as subtle as possible. Further, if you use your eyes or eyebrows for emphasis, never change to some other means during the middle of the conversation. You can be very expressive with a raised eyebrow or a quick side glance at your subject. Practice in front of a mirror sometimes to see just what disbelief, amusement, doubt, honesty, or sincerity look like with eye expression. Practice a little and you will find that facial expression can be a really valuable tool in your interrogation.

VOCAL EXPRESSION

Vocal expression is equally as important, if not more so, than facial expression. Facial acting will not work for many interrogators, but putting feeling in one's voice can be done by everybody.

It is suggested that in the very beginning of your conversation with the subject, you adopt a rather flat, monotone-type voice until you can sense whether the subject is receptive to you or not. I don't mean a flat, singsong-type conversation but more of a no-nonsense tone. After you decide more about this subject and how the conversation is going, then you can introduce more expression into your words.

If you are being firm and positive in your approach, let your words reflect this attitude by containing the proper timbre and strength. Let your words sound as if you will not take No for an answer. Your vocal expression can be as impressive as your words if you only will try and put the proper emphasis on what you are saying. Next time you are in a conversation with some friends, stop and listen to the tones rise and fall as each person in turn reinforces his comments by emphasizing and using his vocal tones in his conversation. If your interrogations include the rise and fall of tone and the proper emphasis on each word, you will be much more effective than the person who does not consider this point in his interrogation preparedness.

Again, do not overemphasize but use enough range in your voice to be believable. If you do not believe the person, and you tell him so, don't mildly say it—come right on out and leave no doubt in his mind that you don't believe him. If you are using the sincere approach, sound sincere just as if you and he are the best buddies ever. It takes a little acting, but it will help you in the long run. You have never heard a good salesman speak of his product mildly; similarly, you cannot sell yourself, or the fact that the person should tell the truth, if you don't speak with belief. Listen to the commercials on TV or radio and you will get a good idea how much vocal expression can add to a few written or spoken words. You might even practice this a little by trying out a few words along with the facial expressions. Practice will make both of these tools useful even if you do feel a little foolish in the beginning.

Above all, never allow boredom to appear in any of your expressions. If the suspect feels he has you on the run, he will do nothing to let you off the hook. If he feels, however, that you are as fresh and ready as ever, he often will decide he might as well come across.

Try to make all of your words achieve about the same value in emphasis when using terms concerning the crime. By emphasizing harsh words, you can oftentimes drive the suspect clear into himself through fear alone. If the harsh words are not emphasized, they do not take on a fearsome or dreadful meaning in the suspect's mind. It is best to substitute some less-threatening word if you can, but if that is impossible, don't give any special emphasis to the harsh words.

In all of this suggested use of vocal and physical expression, the key word is practice. None of these things are any good if they are not included in your bag of tricks and then only if you use them well and smoothly. Practice will give you the edge that you need to present a smooth, believable message from the group of words that you have at your command.

BIBLIOGRAPHY

1. Dudycha, George: *Psychology for Law Enforcement Officers.* Springfield, Thomas, 1955.
2. Inbau, Fred E. and Reid, John E.: *Criminal Interrogation and Confessions,* 2nd ed. Baltimore, Williams and Wilkins, 1967.
3. Inbau, Fred E. and Reid, John E.: *Criminal Interrogation and Confessions Study Guide.* Santa Cruz, Davis Publishing Company, 1968.
4. Leonard, V. A.: *Academy Lectures on Lie Detection.* Springfield, Thomas, 1958, vol. 2.
5. McDonald, Hugh C.: *The Practical Psychology of Police Interrogation.* Santa Ana, California, Townsend, 1963.
6. Prochnow, Herbert V.: *The Successful Speaker's Handbook.* Englewood Cliffs, N.J., Prentice-Hall, 1959, p. 34.
7. Reik, Theo: *Compulsion to Confess.* New York, Farrar, Straus and Cudahy, 1959.
8. Rogge, John: *Why Men Confess.* New York, Thomas Nelson and Son, 1959.
9. Weston, Paul B. and Wells, Kenneth M.: *Criminal Investigation—Basic Precepts.* Englewood Cliffs, N.J., Prentice-Hall, 1970.
10. Winters, John: *Crime and Kids.* Springfield, Thomas, 1959.

INDEX

H

Habits of subject, 16
Haircuts, 126
Handwritten statements, 110
Harsh words, 33, 40, 74, 129
Height of subject, 11
Human behavior, 36, 42
Human comforts, 36, 51
Human dignity, 21

I

Impartial attitude, 32-33
Impersonal involvement, 31
Indiscreet remarks, 11
Integrity, 25
Intelligence of subject, 11
Interrogation, history of, 3-4
Interrogation Request Form, 6, 7, 62
Interrogation room, 54
  color, 55
  construction, 55, 56, 57, 58
  furniture, 55, 56, 57
Interrogation techniques, 12, 21, 40,
  46, 52, 60, 75, 78, 87, 97, 101
Interview, definition, 16
Introspection, 46
Investigating officer, 7, 9, 103

J

Juvenile Court records, 17

K

Keep upper hand, 36, 41

L

Leading questions, 107
Leading the conversation, 16
Legal facts, 44
Lying, 8, 21, 38, 57, 81, 97, 98

M

M.O., see Method of operation
Make yourself available, 100, 103
Marathon interrogation, 8
Marital troubles of subject, 14
McDonald, Hugh C., 11, 20

Memorize
  business name, 18
  complainant's name, 18
  evidence, 21
  method of operation, 19
  time and date, 19
  what was taken, 19
  witnesses, 20
Mental preparation, 23
Method of operation, 19-20, 83
Miranda decision warning, 45, 50, 72,
  79, 108, 113, 114
Motivation, 9
Mugging and printing information, 9

N

Nervous habits, 31
Nervousness of interrogator, 76
Noise, 54
Note taking, 47, 82

O

Observation mirror, 57
Occupation of subject, 12
"One more time," 96, 101
One page written statements, 105
"Open door" closing, 100, 103
Opening statement, 73, 76
Organized thinking, 36, 37
Outside distractions, 54
Outside pressure, 36, 39
Over talking, 30

P

Patience, 76, 92
Patronizing, 36, 46
"Pedigree" sheet, 9, 10, 67
Personal odor, 126
Personal property, 15
Personality of interrogator, 24, 34
Personality of subject, 20, 70
Photographing information, 9
Physical attributes, 11
Physical violence, 51
Place of birth, 12
Place of business interrogation, 60
Playing the part, 32
Police car interrogation, 59
Police equipment, 36, 39, 125

Police records, 14
Posture, 126
Preconceived ideas, 36, 39
Prejudice, 27
Preliminary preparation, 9
Previous interrogation, 8, 15
Pride, subject's, 12
Privacy, 54, 60
Prochnow, Herbert V., 26
Profanity, 28, 112
Profession of subject, 12
Professional attitude, 29, 37
Promises, 36, 49, 110, 111
Proper dress, 124
Prudence, 43, 52

R

Race of subject, 8
Realistic words, 36, 40
Referring to crime, 75
Relating the conversation, 36, 38
Relatives of subject, 16
Religion, 13
Resentment, subject's, 14
Ridicule, 17

S

Self analysis, 33
Self respect, 24, 51
Sequencing actions, 81
Shackles, 36, 41
Shyness, interrogator, 11, 31, 32
Sitting close, 36, 40
Slang, 27
Sleep, subject's, 8
Smoking, 36, 41
Social position of subject, 16, 36, 49
Sources of information, 93
Stenographer, 108
Street interrogation, 60
Surprise at admission, 36, 47, 94
Sympathetic approach, juvenile, 17
Sympathy, 48

T

Tape recording, 108
Teenagers, 17
Temper, 24

Thoughts of subject, 9
Threats, 36, 44, 50
Time, 42, 76
Time element, 20, 81, 82, 85, 88, 91, 92
Traffic violations records, 14
Two page written statements, 117
Typographical errors in statements, 112

U

Unlawful confession, 44
Unsuccessful interrogation, 99

V

Vocabulary, 26
Vocabulary of interrogator, 13
Vocal expression, 128, 129
Voluntary confession, 44

W

Weight of subject, 11
Where to interrogate, 54
Withholding information, 88, 91
Witnesses, 16, 20, 69, 87, 92, 93
Written statement
  closing of, 115
  coaching, 106
  Constitutional rights in, 113, 114
  contents, 105
  exact words in, 112
  example, 117-118
  final question, 109
  heading of, 108, 113, 114
  initialing, 112, 114, 121
  Miranda decision warnings, 108
  opening of, 108
  profanity in, 112
  question and answer type, 106
  reading aloud, 121
  signing of, 115
  single spacing of, 111
  typing of, 110
  "yes" and "no" questions, 107
  witnesses signing of, 115, 116

Y

"Yes" and "no" questions, 73, 92, 107